A Melody Too Sweet to Forget

JoAnn and Robert DeSilva
With
Sandi Huddleston-Edwards

Published by Hear My Heart Publishing

Copyright 2020
Written by Sandi Huddleston-Edwards

ISBN: 978-1-945620-74-4

A product of the United States of America. Written by Sandi Huddleston-Edwards

This book is a work of non-fiction.

Dedication

"Rejoice in hope, endure in affliction, persevere in prayer."
Romans 12:12 (NABRE)

With sincere appreciation, Bob and I dedicate this book to the many music, choral, and drama students taught by our daughter, JoAnna Rosalie DeSilva Berggren. You filled her heart and soul with joy and warmth in ways no others could. In addition to her love for God, family, and friends, she deeply loved her students.

JoAnna enjoyed being a music teacher at Boyle Road Elementary School because of your genuine desire to learn, your eagerness to incorporate music into your young lives, and your summoned courage to perform. These were all the rewards she ever desired. Even though her days were cut short, her life was lived in harmony and selflessness. Her zest for life was fed by making people happy and from your acceptance and unblemished desire to learn about music.

Music was JoAnna's passion whether she was hearing it, singing it, playing it, reading it, dancing to it, or teaching it. We had the pleasure and privilege of attending many of the excellent concerts and amazing performances she directed and you presented as young children. Along with your smiles and well-deserved pride were bright eyes of devotion and respect for your teacher. JoAnna treasured your new-found abilities and well-earned successes.

Thank you for sharing JoAnna's contagious enthusiasm and God-given musical talents to unlock new doors and possibilities in your lives. Your affections colored her world with a brilliance that overflowed from the depths of her heart. She would have been touched by the outpouring of tenderness you shared sixteen years ago and the lasting memories you continue to share.

JoAnna's life was a sweet melody – one that doesn't come along too often. But when it does, it is a melody that can never be forgotten. Thank you for singing her song.

Acknowledgements

"Call to me, and I will answer you; I will tell you great things beyond the reach of your knowledge."
Jeremiah 33:3 (NABRE)

With our deepest love and genuine pride, we would like to express our sincere gratitude to our children Robert (Bobby) DeSilva, Angela DeSilva Zippel, and Annmarie DeSilva Marchisotto. We are so blessed to be your parents. We value each of your unique gifts, talents and skills, and different displays of devotion and love.

Over the years, you have showered us with laughter, triumphs, and celebrations. During the times when it has seemed too difficult to take another step, you have been there to speak words of wisdom and encouragement even though you were hurting yourselves. You have emboldened our strength with warm hugs, welcome telephone calls, and kisses on the cheeks. We cherish our large family -- your spouses, our grandchildren, and our great-grandchildren -- who brighten our days.

And we especially want to thank you for sharing your poignant memories of JoAnna, so this book can come to fruition after sixteen long years. Our hope is this book will keep her memory alive and inspire others to live their lives to the fullest as she had done.

It's difficult to express how much we love you, but this famous poem by Henry Wadsworth Longfellow does a good job. God bless you always.

Mom and Dad (JoAnn and Bob DeSilva)

The Children's Hour
Henry Wadsworth Longfellow

Between the dark and the daylight,
When the night is beginning to lower,
Comes a pause in the day's occupations,
That is known as the Children's Hour.
I hear in the chamber above me
The patter of little feet,
The sound of a door that is opened,
And voices soft and sweet.

From my study I see in the lamplight,
Descending the broad hall stair,
Grave Alice, and laughing Allegra
And Edith with golden hair.

A whisper, and then a silence:
Yet I know by their merry eyes
They are plotting and planning together
To take me by surprise.

A sudden rush from the stairway,
A sudden raid from the hall!
By three doors left unguarded
They enter my castle wall!

They climb up into my turret
O'er the arms and back of my chair;
If I try to escape, they surround me;
They seem to be everywhere.

They almost devour me with kisses,
Their arms about me entwine,
Till I think of the Bishop of Bingen
In his Mouse-Tower on the Rhine!

Do you think, O blue-eyed banditti,
Because you have scaled the wall,
Such an old mustache as I am
Is not a match for you all!

I have you fast in my fortress,
And will not let you depart,
But put you down into the dungeon
In the round-tower of my heart.

And there will I keep you forever,
Yes, forever and a day,
Till the walls shall crumble to ruin,
 And moulder in dust away!

Table of Contents

A Note to Readers

"I command you: be strong and steadfast!
Do not fear nor be dismayed,
for the LORD, your God,
is with you wherever you go."
Joshua 1:9 (NABRE)

It was a lovely warm September evening at Birkdale Village in Huntersville, North Carolina, the kind that makes you sad the summer season is on the downside. Schools and colleges were back in session; vacations and summer trips to the North and South Carolina beaches were ending; and fall was being heralded in with hints of red, orange, and yellow colors mingled among the leaves of deciduous trees. The retail stores, coffee houses, and restaurants, which lined both sides of the street, were quiet, almost empty. As my husband was about to grab the door handle of our favorite bistro, my cell phone rang. The display indicated the call was from an *Unknown Number* in Florida. Normally, I don't answer these calls and think, *If it's important, the caller will leave a voice mail message.* Besides, my empty stomach was growling and my husband was frowning. But for whatever reason, I chose to answer the call. I pressed the button. "Hello?"

A lady's voice with a strong New York accent asked, "Are you Sandi Huddleston-Edwards, the lady who wrote Kelly Spence Cain's book?"

"Yes, ma'am. She and I worked on her book together."

"My name is JoAnn DeSilva. I read Kelly's book and liked it very much. She gave me your phone number and suggested I talk with you. You see, I want to know if you'll write a book about my daughter, JoAnna, who died in 2004. My daughter was only twenty-nine years-old and such a beautiful girl whom everybody loved. I can't name anyone who didn't love my daughter. She was special."

"JoAnn, I only write Christian genre."

"I know. We're Christians. We're Catholics. JoAnna was a very special person. I believe in my heart she was a true angel on earth, and I want people to learn about her goodness. I want JoAnna remembered and not forgotten. I want people to know how she led her life helping others."

I had received several calls like this one in the past and had realized the romantic desire of "writing a book" can be strong, but in the end, it can become a fleeting moment – a temporary desire, which fizzles out after you discuss documenting a book proposal and query letter, my writing fees, time and research involved, acquiring a publisher, contracts, and other items. As I gave her the one minute "elevator speech" regarding these requirements, she remained interested, asking a few questions. I realized she wasn't being dissuaded in the least. Actually, she seemed even more determined to have this book written about her daughter, JoAnna. I also could detect lingering pain and ongoing grief in her voice even after fourteen years since JoAnna's death. We scheduled a follow-up phone conversation for the following week and wished each other a good night.

During dinner, I pondered why I had answered this call from an *unknown number*, especially because my husband and I were both hungry, and I usually waited to hear a voice message. I also was telling myself, *I'm already working on two books and have contracts to write two others. Do I really want to take on another book right now? Will JoAnn still be interested when I call back? Will I be interested after talking with her some more?*

Over the next few days, I couldn't forget JoAnn's request to write a book about her daughter. Her passion and determination for the world to know her daughter was almost pleading. As a mother, I could understand why she wanted to keep her daughter's memory alive. I'd do the same if I were her. That is when I knew what had captured me: We both had mothers' hearts. Over hundreds of miles from Florida to North Carolina and over cyber waves, we had connected. We were kindred spirits joined together by the undying, enormous amount of love we had for our children. Not only did we have a bond with our children, we had relationships with God. He had blessed both of us with a magnificent gift: motherhood. After praying, I felt God wanted this book to be written in memory of JoAnna Rosalie DeSilva Berggren.

Maya Angelou once stated, "I write to be closer to God." Like Angelou, I write for the glory of God, as well. I am humbled and grateful to God for the special people and their inspirational stories whom He has placed in my path. He had blessed me again.

"JoAnn, if you're still interested, I want to help you write JoAnna's book. Hopefully, my publisher, Beth S. Wilson, of Hear My Heart Publishing, will accept our book proposal. What do you want to do?"

"Oh, good! Thank you, Sandi. I want us to write this book."

Then JoAnn yelled to her husband. "Bob! She's going to write JoAnna's book! He said, 'Good.' We're both excited. I don't want anyone to forget JoAnna or not to realize there are good people like her in this world. I don't want to write this book to make a lot of money, but any money that is made will be given to a scholarship fund that was created in our daughter's honor."

"That is truly altruistic, JoAnn. I believe this will be a special book and one God has ordained to be written." Then I changed direction. "Could you tell me about JoAnna?"

"Sure, and I agree with you. I believe God wants this book written. I've thought about it for a long time. My daughter, JoAnna, was a devout Catholic. JoAnna only lived twenty-nine years, but she lived her life according to her Christian faith. I want people to know there are good people in the world who make a difference and touch others in special ways. I want to encourage them to become one of those people like JoAnna was. I'm tired of reading about bad people and hearing about bad people in the news. I think people want to read about good people. JoAnna was a good person."

That night, I marveled about how easy it had been to write the book proposal and query letter. JoAnn had given this book much thought over the years since her daughter's death. I couldn't wait to email the documents to my publisher, Beth S. Wilson. On October 18, 2018, she gave us her decision.

Beth wrote, "JoAnn, thank you for considering Hear My Heart Publishing. It would be my honor to publish this precious book. I pray the writing of this manuscript will bring healing and joy as you go through the process. You are in good hands with Sandi.... Trust her. Let her guide you in this process."

I can't explain how blessed I felt (and still do) about having a Christian publisher who believed in the stories that God had presented for me to write. God had surely blessed me again and was now blessing JoAnn with Beth's decision to publish JoAnna's book. This young woman's short life would be chronicled in written words that would, hopefully, touch the hearts of many people, leading them to have a relationship with God and to live their lives as fully and as memorably as this remarkable woman had done. My journey of discovering more about JoAnna's life began that night.

The following months were spent making phone calls, leaving messages, sending emails, conducting telephone interviews, and reading documents, articles, and letters about JoAnna. Her friends and family members had even shared poignant emotions, some that had been stored away and safely guarded in their hearts. Some reminiscences were recalled that they hadn't tapped into for fourteen years. They hadn't allowed themselves to. My recordings and notes created an invisible album with imaginary photographs of a lovely young woman with long black hair, ivory skin, and a constant smile. The innumerable faux pages held a collection of treasured memories when her fleeting reality had touched their lives and even the lives of strangers.

I was privileged to learn about a beautiful young woman, who was referred to as *the glue who kept the family together*. She was cherished as a wife, daughter, sister, sister-in-law, aunt, niece, teacher, and friend. They talked of their *JoJo* as if they had just seen her. She enjoyed eating ice cream and pasta, making people laugh, and showing others where to find rainbows after every dark and bursting cloud. In her twenty-nine years and seven months of life, this dedicated teacher had impressed her graciousness on countless students' hearts and left positive indelible impressions as gifts for a lifetime. No one had forgotten her – they couldn't forget someone so unique and so deeply loved. She was a rare jewel in the midst of many; she was exemplary, kind, giving, and loving.

JoAnna had many loves. Her first love was Christ and the church. She loved attending church on Sundays and being a cantor for Mass and a choir director for the children's Mass. She openly displayed genuine love for her husband, parents, siblings, other family members, co-workers, and friends by making them feel valued and important in her life. She loved music – playing the piano and singing with her beautiful soprano voice. She loved teaching music, drama, and chorus to her K - 5th grade students. She loved being surrounded by people and used each opportunity to spread joy and encouragement to all. She loved everything *Betty Boop*, proudly tattooing her ankle and decorating her bedroom and classroom with the cartoon character. In short, JoAnna loved her life.

Now don't get this wrong. JoAnna was human and imperfect. None are perfect but the One Who walked this earth as a human being, the One Who never sinned, yet He died on a rugged cross, and the One Who defeated death by rising again. Because of the way JoAnna lived her life, it's a true blessing and honor to write this memoir about a young woman, who many people describe as *an angel on earth.*

My prayer is that readers will receive inspirational messages of hope, faith, and love throughout these pages and will be motivated to live their lives as JoAnna did in compliance with Jesus' new commandment in John 13:34-35 (ESV):

"A new commandment I give to you, that you love one another: just as I have loved you, you also are to love one another. By this all people will know that you are my disciples, if you have love for one another."

JoAnn's prayer is "Hopefully, after reading about my daughter, readers will say, 'Look at what an impact this one person was able to do with her life by being kind and good and loving.'"

JoAnna Rosalie DeSilva Berggren left behind a legacy of love for the privileged people who knew her and even for those who didn't. Simply, JoAnna was love incarnate.

Sandi Huddleston-Edwards

Prologue

"I have told you this so that you might have peace in me.
In the world you will have trouble, but take courage,
I have conquered the world."
John 16:33 (NABRE)

A Melody Too Sweet To Forget

WHY...WHY...WHY? How many times must we cry for our children that have been senselessly taken away. JoAnna Berggren's young life was snuffed out by a random, brutal act of greed and stupidity. Her family, with whom we have been associated for many years, is a good family, a caring, loving and giving family. In the blink of an eye a precious jewel, a beautiful, healthy, vibrant young woman was viciously killed, leaving her young bridegroom to be widowed, her parents without their child, her siblings without their sister and a whole community without a remarkable woman.

JoAnna was a talented musician, singer and teacher. Even for her young age she gave so much to so many people and touched the lives of the most important and most impressionable – the children. Her students came by the carload, sobbing and weeping for the loss of that one special teacher that strikes a special chord in all our lives.

The family, so devasted by this loss, could barely withstand their emotional pain. Her mother, so crushed by the death of her daughter wept from the depths of her soul, her body racked with sobbing. Her father and siblings valiantly carried the burden of greeting each and every person whose life Joanna had in some small measure affected. They came by the hundreds to say farewell, to mourn such a good person, such a special person. Her young husband, physically injured, could not deaden the pain in his heart for his beautiful beloved wife and what their lives would have been together.

"She was the rock of our family" said her sobbing brother. "She was so special" echoed her aunt. The beautiful, vibrant young woman, so full of life and promise of what would be tomorrow lies there in her casket. Her classic beauty framed by long, raven black tresses on alabaster skin almost defied the eye to accept her death. Out of such a tragic death came the peace of a soul gone to Heaven and the fulfillment of Paradise.

Standing in procession came her devoted little students, each with a perfect red carnation; they presented their prize to their beloved mentor and tears flowed down their cherub faces.

Your sweet voice and caring ways will be missed so deeply by all who knew you, JoAnna. The dreams of your future can now only be seen in the recesses of our hearts and souls. You are now director [for] a choir of angels for the glory of God and may your music fill our every waking hour . . . sweet dreams dear, JoAnna.

This article was written by Barbara Guarino Kruk, posted on February 11, 2004, and provided
by Robert DeSilva, JoAnna's father.
(It is printed here with Ms. Kruk's permission.)

JoAnna Rosalie DeSilva Berggren
June 6, 1974 – January 31, 2004

"Blessed are the peacemakers,
for they will be called children of God."
Matthew 5:9 (NABRE)

A Purpose for Living

"For we are his handiwork, created in Christ Jesus for the good
works that God has prepared in advance,
that we should live in them."
Ephesians 2:10 (NABRE)

Scriptures tell us God has given each of us a purpose for life that
we are to fulfill. God knows everything about us, even the number
of hairs on our heads (Matthew 10:20, NABRE). We're not here
by coincidence or accident. We're here because God formed us
in His image, each a unique creation to serve His purpose – not
our own. Some people discover their purpose early in life; others
don't discover theirs until later in life. And tragically, after lonely
and empty-handed quests, some people never discover theirs.

The Bible records in Jeremiah 1:4-5 (NABRE) the moment
when Jeremiah was called by God to be a prophet. "The word of
the Lord came to me: 'Before I formed you in the womb I knew
you, before you were born I dedicated you, a prophet to the
nations I appointed you.'"

In addition to a purpose, God has given each of us a spirit not
of fear but of power, love, and self-control, as well as affording us
talents to fulfill each purpose. Our sinful lives on this earth do not
last forever. We are told only "if you confess with your mouth that
Jesus is Lord and believe in your heart that God raised him from
the dead, you will be saved" (Romans 10:9, NABRE) and given
eternal life. "For the wages of sin is death, but the gift of God is
eternal life in Christ Jesus our Lord" (Romans 6:23, NABRE).

The Holy Spirit gives us fruit of the spirit as told in Galatians
5:22-23 (NABRE). "In contrast, the fruit of the Spirit is love, joy,
peace, patience, kindness, generosity, faithfulness, gentleness,

self-control. Against such **the**re is no law."

Therefore, each person should approach his/her life with faithfulness, obedience, and determination to discover God's purpose and direction and to work toward fulfilling His purpose. Our days are numbered, so we should pray as David did. "Teach us to count our days aright, that we may gain wisdom of heart" (Psalm 90:12, NABRE). "Now David, after he had served the will of God in his lifetime, fell asleep, was gathered to his ancestors, and did see corruption" (Acts 13:36, NABRE).

Have you known people who seem to be joyful or happy all the time? What exactly is *joy*? According to Dictionary.com, **joy** is "the emotion of great delight or happiness caused by something exceptionally good or satisfying." These joyful people seem to always see the world through an optimistic *glass half full* lens and are never overly bothered or frustrated by unexpected changes or detours. They just adapt. It's like they have a clear direction of their goal and how to get there. Some folks may label these people as *too good to be true*. Maybe they are, and again, maybe they are not. Maybe they've made a discovery of something exceptionally good or satisfying. So, for the few whom you deem genuine and authentic, from where does their never-ending joy and positive disposition come?

According to Fred Bittner in the article, "Bible Verses About Joy: 25 Scriptures on Happiness," a sub-title reads, "Joy comes when we have a clear direction for our life" (*FaithGateway.com*), Bittner even invites us to exchange the word *direction* with the word *purpose*. He bases his belief of acquiring joy in Psalm 16:11 (NABRE): "You will show me the path to life, abounding joy in your presence, the delights at your right hand forever."

Once we recognize our purpose for living, there is no more energy and stress in searching for its discovery. Instead, we can begin the actual work of living and preparing ourselves through practice, education, and knowledge to fulfill our life's objective. And along the way, we can strive to become more like Jesus by acquiring and / or honing the nine characteristics of the fruit of the Holy Spirit.

JoAnn and Bob DeSilva, who are devout Christians and dedicated parents, took faithful and obedient steps to ensure their children developed strong Christian foundations. Based on what is known about JoAnna Rosalie DeSilva Berggren, it's easy for me to believe she was one of those fortunate people who had discovered life's *purpose / direction* at a young age. Perhaps, her sensitive, precocious nature had led her to an early perception of God's grace and mercy. It's easy to apply Bittner's thesis about *joy* in order to suggest the source of JoAnna's constant joyful disposition. If she discovered her purpose early on, then she had been released from the burden of searching for it. Instead, she was able to rejoice in its discovery and concentrate on the necessary steps, correct choices, and untraveled pathways to fulfill God's purpose for her life.

"...she was one of those happily created beings who please without effort, make friends everywhere, and take life so gracefully and easily that less fortunate souls are tempted to believe that such are born under a lucky star."

Louisa May Alcott, *Little Women*

As a Child, She was Special

"You are the light of the world. A city set on a mountain cannot be hidden. Nor do they light a lamp and then put it under a bushel basket; it is set on a lampstand, where it gives light to all in the house. Just so, your light must shine before others, that they may see your good deeds and glorify your heavenly Father."
Matthew 5:14-16 (NABRE)

JoAnn DeSilva (Mother)

God blessed Bob and me with four healthy children for which we are eternally grateful. We did our best to raise them well and with the fundamental beliefs of the church. Each of our children has qualities and attributes, which are different, just as each of them has qualities and attributes, which are similar. Our children were raised in a harmonious home, where (my husband) their father worked hard, travelling hours to get to work in New York City and travelling hours to return home. These long commutes added to the normal work hours made for a long, tiresome day. My job was to keep the home fires burning by ensuring our children were fed and clothed and given opportunities to blossom and grow. We love our children very much, but because this book is about our third child, JoAnna Rosalie DeSilva Berggren, we'll focus on her remarkable life.

JoAnna was born June 6, 1974. Carrying her for nine months, along with my labor and delivery, were much easier compared to giving birth to my first two children. When our beautiful baby was one month and a few days old, her Baptism was held on July 14, 1974, in St. Jude Catholic Church in Mastic Beach, Long Island, New York. Our first-born, Robert (Bobby), and our second child, Angela, had been baptized and took their sacraments in St. Rita's Roman Catholic Church, Astoria, Queens, New York. Later, their marriages took place in St. Jude. JoAnna and our youngest daughter, Annmarie, were baptized and took all of their sacraments in St. Jude.

As a small child, JoAnna had a joyful spirit. She smiled a lot, seemed contented, and never got upset and threw temper tantrums when something bothered her or didn't go her way. Throughout the years, she was a good kid and grew to be a good person. JoAnna had a wonderful personality. Even when she was a small girl, people described her as having an ever-present smile on her pretty face. Early on, Bob and I noticed that our daughter went out of her way to make other people happy or to bring peace to a troublesome situation or quarreling individuals. We marveled at her patient and gentle manner that was displayed to everyone she encountered – those she knew and those who were strangers. It became obvious people were attracted to her as if she were a magnet. She drew them close and conquered them with kindness and taking a genuine interest in their lives. Our daughter possessed the most calming demeanor of anyone I've ever known.

JoAnna took Holy Communion on May 8, 1982, when she was almost eight years old. An interest she expressed early on was the desire to take piano lessons, so we purchased a piano for her, and she took lessons from Madame Pringle, our church organist. Later, Madame Pringle began giving JoAnna voice lessons. At the age of ten, Madame Pringle brought JoAnna to church to sing a solo on Christmas Eve. She believed JoAnna was that gifted. One day, Madame Pringle told us, "When JoAnna sings, she should be able to accompany herself on the piano." So, JoAnna learned how to play the piano and sing at the same time.

Then our daughter surprised her father and me when she expressed an interest in singing in the church choir, so we readily agreed. We had always encouraged our children to pursue their interests, so we wanted JoAnna to have the opportunity to fulfill this desire. Over the several years when JoAnna sang in the church choir, she developed a beautiful voice. Believe it or not, neither Bob nor I ever had to remind JoAnna to take her lessons. It wasn't long before Bob and I shared the belief that JoAnna's lovely voice and strong piano skills were God-given talents. She excelled in her music.

When JoAnna was sixteen, she made Confirmation on March 30, 1991. She really touched my heart when she chose my mother as her Confirmation Sponsor. Mother was extremely honored and considered it a privilege to be asked by JoAnna to serve in this life-long role. The purpose of Confirmation is that it "connects and strengthens a person's bond with the holy spirit" (scripturecatholic. com). Not only would Mother participate in the ceremony, but she would make a solemn oath to offer support and guidance for JoAnna "[t]o guide her into adulthood, and to give her the skills needed to face the challenges in life and to help strengthen her faith in God and the church." This sincere commitment is never to be taken lightly because it is "to help guide and influence another soul" (scripturecatholic.com). JoAnna would take my mother's name as her middle name. My mother's name was *Rosalie* and with JoAnna's middle name already being *Rosalie*, there was no notable change.

Because of her love for church, music, and children, she started the children's choir at church. There were many children who participated.

JoAnna was a gregarious person by nature, who basked in being surrounded by people – lots of people. She wasn't afraid to speak in a large group or perform in front of an audience. Our daughter thrived in making people feel special and appreciated. It was obvious to us and others, JoAnna was born with a big heart and enjoyed seeing other people happy. Perhaps, she really had recognized her purpose in life early on and was working passionately to fulfill it, mindful of an internal hour glass that couldn't be seen.

Summary

- Recognition each child was different and similar from the others.
- Her children were raised in a harmonious home.
- Her children were raised with a Christian foundation.
- JoAnna had a big heart and enjoyed seeing other people happy.
- At an early age, it is thought she had discovered her purpose in life.

She worked diligently to fulfill her purpose.

Only A Dad
by Edgar Guest

Only a dad, with a tired face,
Coming home from the daily race,
Bringing little of gold or fame,
To show how well he has played the game,
But glad in his heart that his own rejoice
To see him come, and to hear his voice.

Only a dad, with a brood of four,
One of ten million men or more.
Plodding along in the daily strife,
Bearing the whips and the scorns of life,
With never a whimper of pain or hate,

For the sake of those who at home await.
Only a dad, neither rich nor proud,
Merely one of the surging crowd
Toiling, striving from day to day,
Facing whatever may come his way,

Silent, whenever the harsh condemn,
And bearing it all for the love of them.
Only a dad, but he gives his all
To smooth the way for his children small,
Doing, with courage stern and grim,
The deeds that his father did for him.
This is the line that for him I pen,
Only a dad, but the best of men.

As a Daughter,
She Was Full of Surprises

"Charm is deceptive and beauty fleeting;
the woman who fears the LORD IS TO BE PRAISED.
Acclaim her for the work of her hands,
and let her deeds praise her at the city gates."
Proverbs 31:30-31 (NIV)

Robert (Bob) DeSilva (Father)

I was born in New York, technically Long Island, to a Mexican father and an Irish mother. Sometime throughout the years, our ancestors had changed the name *Silva* to *DeSilva*. My mother's maiden name was Pero. Her ancestors were mostly Irish, but their surname was Italian. Originally, their name had been *DePiero* or *Dipiero* until ancestors changed it / shortened it to *Pero*.

I remember my mother always singing and playing the piano. She didn't have the advantages my daughter would have. When my mother was very young, her mother died. In order to care for the children, my grandfather had to place his children in a home for children. In those days, they were known as orphanages. Unfortunately, my mother's little sister died while she was living in the children's home. It was a sad time for Mother and her siblings. Later after Mother was grown and left the home, she would go to my aunt's home (her sister) to play the piano. My mother always sang and played the piano, but as I said, she didn't have the advantages my daughter, JoAnna, did.

When I was sixteen years old and JoAnn was fourteen or fifteen, we met for the first time. My sister knew JoAnn's sister, but we didn't know each other, and we didn't attend the same

6

school. When I first saw her, I told my friend, "She's interesting." And she was. She was different from anyone I'd ever met. She had different colored hair that now I would say reminded me of a *punk rocker*.

"I want to meet her," I said.

"Are you sure?" was his response.

"Yes."

So, I met JoAnn on my own, and we began dating. Our relationship was rocky, like most teenagers, and we'd break up for a little while and then go back together. JoAnn is a very talented artist, so naturally, her parents wanted her to attend Art School. However, JoAnn was stubborn and didn't want to go. I quit high school and attended night school to earn my diploma, which I did. Eventually, we decided we wanted to be with each other, so we got married on October 25, 1962, when she was nineteen, and I was twenty-one. My intentions were to go to college, but because I was married by this time, we needed the money.

We first lived in an apartment in Astoria, Queens, New York. From there we moved to a very nice housing project and then moved to Long Island in 1972. This is where we lived when JoAnna and Annmarie were born. My son, Bobby, and my daughter, Angela, had been born in Astoria. I worked in New York City for NYTel (Baby Bell), which was part of AT&T at that time. For fourteen or fifteen years, I commuted to the city. It took two hours and ten minutes for me to get to work and another two hours and ten minutes for me to get home. It was incredible. Because our family was growing, I worked all the hours I could to earn extra money. Unfortunately, the company had lots of strikes over the years. Sometimes, when I stopped working for the day, it was too late to travel home, so I would stay with my in-laws in Astoria.

Finally, I was given a transfer to Long Island, reducing my total commute time four hours and six minutes. When we moved out there, it took me ten to fourteen minutes to get to the garage. It was terrific! I had so much extra time on my hands no longer having to ride to and from work in the City. It was hard to decide what to do with all of it.

I'll never forget the night JoAnna was born. When I took my wife to the hospital, everything went really well. There was a certain sense that every aspect of her birth was happening in sync. The first time I saw my baby girl, it was magical. I remember that later when I was driving home, it wasn't quite daylight yet. The stars seemed very bright and were twinkling. They seemed to be so close, I could reach up and grab them. I turned on the car radio, and what did I hear? It was the song, "The Apple of My Eye," by Stevie Wonder, which seemed so appropriate for the occasion; it couldn't have been better. Everything in JoAnna's life seemed to be the same way – in sync and couldn't have been better.

As JoAnna grew, she looked like a small version of her mother. She was a little shorter and her features were somewhat darker. Even though her hair was naturally a dark brown, she dyed her hair black. We recognized that she was a talented young girl when, as a little kid, she expressed an interest in taking piano lessons and singing. She seemed to love music of all types. So, JoAnn and I bought her a baby grand piano, which was second-hand, from a music teacher. The organist / piano player at our church gave JoAnna piano lessons. The lady also sang opera, so she gave JoAnna voice lessons, as well. Later, JoAnna would decide she wanted a new upright piano, so she basically paid for it herself.

After the girls were older, my wife, JoAnn, got a job at the YMCA as a lifeguard. She's a terrific swimmer. She kept this job until our son, Bobby, was going through a divorce and had been awarded custody of his children. So, JoAnn quit her job and went to his home every morning for a few years to keep his kids while he worked.

When our daughter, JoAnna, was nine or ten, there was going to be a father / daughter dance at school. I was somewhat reluctant about going, but she had this gumption and sort of dragged me to the dance. My daughter was always full of surprises. At the age of eight or ten, she sang at the midnight Mass, and the attendees loved it. Obviously, they recognized her talents, and many of those folks encouraged her to continue with the music lessons, which she did. Eventually, as JoAnna got older, she became the children's choir director for early Mass. The kids loved her. She also was the cantor for regular Sunday Mass. After she'd sing, she'd leave the altar and come to where her mother and I were seated to greet us with a kiss. Then she'd return to the altar. This recognition touched our hearts greatly.

You will think this is incredible, but we never had to discipline JoAnna. We never had to tell her to do her homework or practice her piano lessons. She just did them both. Parents of multiple children have to realize each child is unique and has different needs and strengths. One child may need more attention; one child may need independence. But the one thing all children have in common is the need to be loved.

I enjoy cooking and used to make our family's Sunday meal. Our favorite dish was an Italian sauce, meatballs, and macaroni – the whole nine yards. My mother-in-law had taught me how to fix it. I enjoyed experimenting with different spices in the sauce to constantly improve it. And to set the atmosphere, I'd play Italian music on the radio. One of my cherished compliments came from my mother-in-law when she said, "You cook better than I do." Of course, I refrained from agreeing with her. These Sunday meals when we were all together are special memories.

When JoAnna entered high school, she carried her passion for music and drama with her. She was very theatrical and always gave her mother and me tickets to Broadway. We saw *Cats* three times and *Les Misérables* twice. She loved to go to the theater and wanted us to accompany her. We enjoyed these outings, too.

All too soon, it was time for JoAnna to go away to college. She had a hard time leaving home. I remember she threw up all the way the day we drove her. Once she was settled in, she was fine being away from home. We missed her greatly, but I understood kids wanting to be on their own. I'd gone away to summer camp when I was young and had loved every minute of the weeks I attended over the years. It was a carefree week without Mother and Father. Children need space and responsibility in order to grow.

JoAnna called herself a *daddy's girl,* so I guess you could say she was. For one of the solos she sang in a college performance, she had selected "Daddy's Girl," to sing, which warmed my heart deeply. I was extremely proud of her.

Another favorite memory of mine is when I had the honor of walking JoAnna down the aisle of St. Jude Church to give her away. She was a beautiful bride, and it was a lovely wedding. Our priest conducted the ceremony. It seemed that everyone came, as the church and reception were full of well-wishers. She sang "The Wedding Song" during the ceremony, and then she and Jimmy, our son-in-law, sang a song that Jimmy had written entitled, "After the Fall." They had made a CD, which was given as a gift and memento to all attendees. JoAnna's voice couldn't have been any lovelier than it was that day in August 2003.

After I retired from working, I was still in the habit of rising early. JoAnna would be getting ready to leave for work. This gave us a few minutes together. One morning, out of nowhere, she said, "Daddy, thank you for giving me this wonderful life." I don't know what made her say that, but it touched me greatly. I've never heard another person say anything like that. JoAnna was constantly full of surprises. That's the kind of person she was.

JoAnna sang "The Star Spangled Banner" each year at the Boyle Road Elementary grade progression (graduation) ceremony. She also sang "The Star Spangled Banner" for the Ducks' Minor League baseball team on Long Island. The team had wanted to make her a permanent fixture for their home games, but, of course, it didn't happen.

It was extremely difficult to live through the tragedy. We turned to prayer, which is how we got by. I had to do things I didn't think I'd ever be able to do, but I wanted to be strong for my family and my daughter's memory. At the time, JoAnn was unable to go to the courtroom with me, but I was supported by Angela, her husband, Bob, and my son, Bobby, as well as a lot of family and friends who loved JoAnna. It was hard to keep my emotions in check because I didn't want to be emotional. I definitely give God credit for getting us through it. Actually, when I began reading the manuscript of this book, I couldn't get too far into it before I told myself, "I can't read anymore right now."

There were so many nice things done in memory of our daughter. A star was named for her, and a tree was planted in her name. A scholarship fund was created, and playground equipment was purchased and dedicated to her memory. In the middle of winter, the teachers and faculty at her school planned a show, a fundraiser for the scholarship fund. Everyone attended. They even incorporated Betty Boop, her favorite character. It was heart-warming to learn how much she was loved. All the things done in honor of my daughter are appreciated and remain as favorite memories.

I think of the morning when she thanked me for giving her a wonderful life. When I think of it now, I don't know why she had said something like that, but it was about two weeks before the tragedy happened. My suspicion is she had had a premonition, but then again, JoAnna was always full of surprises.

JoAnn and I feel our daughter's presence around us lots of times. It's comforting and something we've gotten used to experiencing. Sometimes when strange things occur, I'll ask JoAnn, "Did you feel that, too?" or "Did you think that, too?" Whenever we're having this kind of discussion, we'll notice a yellow butterfly appears. I'm not sure if it is the same butterfly each time. Just this morning when I was sitting outside on our screened-in patio, I saw the butterfly. I smiled and said aloud, "I see your butterfly."

Never, have I seen anybody influence adults and children the way JoAnna did at the school where she taught, at church, or anywhere. Every kid had a smile on his / her face. I couldn't make a kid smile if I stood on my head. My daughter had this little girl who had earned the lead part in a play, but the little girl was shy. It was unbelievable how JoAnna was able to elicit a performance from that little girl. She just had a great effect on people. Sometimes when people were rude or unfriendly, it bothered her, so JoAnna would say something positive or kind to change the situation or the person's attitude.

Our priest, who truly loved JoAnna, and, who counseled with JoAnn and me during the darkest time of our lives, said something that I'll never forget. He said, "I have two angels to pray to – my mother and JoAnna."

Summary

- Recognize each child has different needs, and provide them to the best of your ability.
- Encourage and support your children's interests and talents.
- Children need space and responsibility in order to grow.
- We turned to prayer to get us through the difficult times.
- We give God credit for getting us through the dark times.

"To be strong, and beautiful, and go round making music all the time. Yes, she could do that, and with a very earnest prayer Polly asked for the strength of an upright soul, the beauty of a tender heart, the power to make her life a sweet and stirring song, helpful while it lasted, remembered when it died."

Louisa May Alcott, *An Old-Fashioned Girl*

As My Niece, She was Adorable

"So then, while we have the opportunity,
let us do good to all,
but especially to those who belong
to the family of the faith."
Galatians 6:10 (NABRE)

Rosalie (Maternal Aunt)

As a little girl, JoAnna was adorable, the cutest little thing you ever saw. My niece was born in June, and my son was born in August the same year. On the day she was born, I thought, *Wow! She is something else!* And as she grew older, she possessed the sweetest disposition of anyone I've ever known. One of my favorite pictures is of my son, Sal, and JoAnna, when they were both two years old. As cousins, they grew up to have a very close relationship. He served as one of the ushers in JoAnna's wedding. My eldest son, Frankie, and Angela are the same age. Even so, Frankie continues to visit JoAnna's grave, as well as my parents' graves.

Early on, JoAnna loved anything musical and was drawn to the piano. She began taking piano lessons at a young age. She also sang. Over the years, she took voice lessons and developed a beautiful voice. At the age of ten, she began singing in the church. I enjoyed having lots of people tell me they attended Sunday Mass just so they could hear her sing.

My maternal grandmother's name was Rosaria; my mother's name was *Rosalie.* I was named *Rosalie* after my mother. My sister's name is Josephine Antoinette (JoAnn), so JoAnna was named after her mother (my sister), Josephine Antoinette (JoAnn). I remember when my sister, JoAnn, was born in a nearby Catholic hospital. She needed a blood transfusion. Our grandmother, Rosaria, was a very devout Christian, so she instructed our mother to pray to Saint Anne to save the baby's life. So, Mother did. She prayed many a prayer for her baby Josephine's life to be saved, and her prayers were heard and answered. Thankfully, our father's blood was a match, which saved my sister, JoAnn's, life.

Many years later, when my sister's daughter and my niece, JoAnna, made Confirmation, she took my mother's name, Rosalie. My mother was so happy to be chosen as her granddaughter's Confirmation Sponsor. This meant that she could take my mother's name to be her middle name. (But since JoAnna was born JoAnna Rosalie DeSilva, she didn't need to change her middle name after Confirmation.) Even though my husband, Sal, and I didn't live close to my sister's family, JoAnna and I remained close as aunt and niece. It made me proud whenever she looked up to me and sought my advice at different times throughout the years.

If there were ever any conflicts in the family, my niece would be the one to settle them. She'd get right in the middle of it and find a way to de-escalate the situation or to help lead those involved to find a solution. She was definitely a *peacemaker* and really a good one, at that. No one ever questioned her advice; they admired her and did whatever she thought was best for them to do.

JoAnna was always close to her parents, brother, and two sisters, Angela and Annmarie. If there were visitors and it was close to dinner time, she'd just cook enough for everyone to eat. JoAnna included everybody – she never excluded anyone. She made everyone feel welcomed to participate in whatever she was doing. As far as I'm aware, she never had cross words or fought with anyone.

And I can tell you from my viewpoint, her husband adored her. When Billy wanted to propose, instead of planning a private, romantic time to ask her to marry him, he did it in front of the people who loved her the most – family, friends, students, parents, and faculty. In my opinion, it was still romantic and very unique and creative. JoAnna and Billy were the perfect couple.

When my niece was tragically killed by a drunk, drugged man, who ran from the vehicle he'd stolen and the scene that he'd caused, it was horrific. It was difficult to accept reality. I kept hoping it was a terrible nightmare. I was living in Florida at this time, so my niece, JoAnna's older sister, Angela, telephoned me with the bad news. I was devastated and deeply saddened, but I hurried to New York to comfort my sister and Bob. I wanted to be there to offer them any assistance possible. Both my sister and brother-in-law were emotionally wrought. They were unable to select clothing for JoAnna to wear for the wake. Angela and I chose the clothes we thought JoAnna might have chosen for herself. My goal was for her to look natural, as if she were going to work. So, we selected a white sweater and skirt. I even chose her underwear. This was a difficult task for Angela and me to carry out, but there was no one else to do it. I am thankful I had the strength and was able to help my family during this dire time.

I couldn't believe the bumper-to-bumper traffic and the number of people who came to her wake. There were so many vehicles making their way to the funeral home, they had to close the William Floyd Parkway, which is a four-lane road named after a signer of the Declaration of Independence. Closing down the Parkway was unheard of – but it was necessary that night because of the many people who wanted to pay their respects to a wonderful person – our JoAnna. There were all types of people who came that night -- police officers, politicians, students, friends, family members, colleagues, college friends, and even her ex-boyfriends from high school. It seemed that all the children and former students of hers brought flowers or small mementos to place in her casket beside her. Their kindness and love were easily seen – no longer intangible emotions. The outpouring was unreal.

My sister was emotionally unable to go inside the funeral home to view her daughter, so she sat out in the lobby. After ensuring she was okay and my other niece, Annmarie, was there to comfort her, I went inside to view my niece. I thought JoAnna looked good and at peace. Her face had not been touched in the accident. As a passenger, she had sustained fatal injuries to her right side and stomach. She didn't die instantly upon impact; she was lying in her husband's arms when she emitted one single word, "Oh," before taking her last breath and passing from this earth to Heaven.

JoAnna was buried at the same cemetery where my mother and father were laid to rest – Mount Pleasant Cemetery in Long Island. Her grave isn't located far from my parents' graves. I don't visit them often, but my son, Frankie, does. Actually, my son goes whenever he isn't travelling and is in town.

Unfortunately, our family wasn't left alone so we could have time to grieve. This is something else the criminal and naturally inquisitive news media took from us. We don't blame the newspapers, television, and others for wanting to know about the beautiful person JoAnna was and whether or not the criminal had been captured. Everyone who knew her was devastated and shocked that the criminal who killed my niece had not been found. Cowardly, he had run from the scene of the accident without any conscience or remorse. The longer he wasn't identified and apprehended, the longer newspaper and television reporters constantly surrounded us, thrusting their questions and mics in our direction, trying to learn any bits of information we might share. Their questions and probes for information were convincing reminders this tragedy was real and not a terrible dream. If only it were a dream from which we could all awaken.

My sister and brother-in-law's hearts were broken into. It was a horrible time for everyone, knowing this man was on the loose and our JoAnna was gone forever. In his selfish acts of stealing a vehicle, using drugs, driving at high rates of speed, running a stop sign, and running away from the scene and injured people who needed his assistance, he had turned his back and our lives upside down and taken away the life of the beautiful person we all knew and loved.

Before I'd moved to Florida, I had been very involved in politics in New York. I served as Secretary to the City of Brookhaven, New York, a town of 100,000 people. I also served as Secretary to Suffolk County, New York, which was comprised of ten towns. One of the highlights of my career was having JoAnna come to a Republican Party event and sing the "Star Spangled Banner." Her voice blessed a lot of people that day who continued to compliment her and me for having such a great singer in my family. So, I knew lots of people and politicians. In addition, I knew lots of judges, which included the judge who would try this case.

He had never known JoAnna personally, but after he read the innumerable letters that friends, family, students, teachers, faculty, and even strangers had sent to him asking for the criminal to receive the maximum sentence, he had to feel as if he'd known her. In fact, JoAnna's strong spirit and the shared memories of JoAnna, which were conveyed by her friends and relatives, had touched him deeply. That was obvious when the judge was handing down the sentence for this criminal. He actually had tears in his eyes when he delivered the sentence. I will paraphrase what I'm told he said. *"I wish I could give you more time than the law allows because of the life you have taken from this world."*

After I returned to Florida, I suffered a heart attack. Shortly afterward, JoAnn and Bob decided they could no longer live in their home. JoAnna and Billy had moved into the basement apartment at her parents' home after they were married. Now, it seemed that every corner of their house, every room, everywhere shouted JoAnna's name. So, they moved to Florida and now live in the house beside my husband and me.

My sister and Bob were kids when they first met. She was fifteen and he was sixteen or seventeen. They married young; I believe JoAnn was nineteen, and Bob must have been twenty or twenty-one. My brother-in-law, Bob, has always supported my sister in everything she did. I don't know what she'd do without Bob. Actually, I don't know what they'd do without each other.

Sadly, my sister still wears black even sixteen years after JoAnna's death. But Bob has moved on. He wears colors other than black. My heart goes out to my sister and to Bob. It has to be the most tragic thing to experience – that of losing a child.

In my opinion, JoAnna wasn't a mama's girl or a daddy's girl. She was her own person, but if you asked my sister, she'd say, "JoAnna was a mama's girl." If you asked Bob, he'd say, "JoAnna was a daddy's girl." Actually, the truth is JoAnna was everybody's girl. I've never known anyone who could stretch herself in so many directions and touch the hearts of so many people. She was amazing.

It is my belief that my Betty Boop-loving niece continues to watch over her family – especially her distraught mother. I believe there are signs of intervention, which are provided to show that her spirit is still present. Many signs have occurred throughout the years, including the strange appearance of halos and rainbows at unusual times and places. Once when we looked out the door, we saw the biggest rainbow we'd ever seen. Even my son, Sal, saw its unique size. None of us had ever seen a rainbow so big and felt JoAnna had whispered to God, asking Him to send it for us.

I was reading the Bible one day when I saw the name *Joanna* in the Bible. How often do you hear the name Joanna? Not very often, but I thought it was amazing when I read it, so I ran next door to tell my sister about it.

I truly believe my niece, JoAnna Rosalie DeSilva Berggren, was an angel on earth, and I'm thankful God sent her to us. I wrote the following message on her first birthday in Heaven.

Darling JoAnna:
Aunt RoRo and Uncle Sal miss you very much.
You were an angel in life and are certainly one now.

JoAnn and Robert DeSilva

You will always be in our hearts and minds forever.
We will always love you.

Rosalie Russello
June 6, 2004

Summary

- Be good to all, especially the family of faith.
- Don't allow conflict to come between you; search for solutions instead. Become peacemakers.
- Use your talents and skills to bless the lives of many.
- Pray for strength in times of trouble and death so you may be of help to those who need it more.

It's all I have to bring today
by Emily Dickinson

It's all I have to bring today—
This, and my heart beside—
This, and my heart, and all the fields—
And all the meadows wide—
Be sure you count—should I forget
Some one the sum could tell—
This, and my heart, and all the Bees
Which in the Clover dwell.

As a Little Sister, She was the Rock

"Blessed are the peacemakers,
for they will be called children of God."
Matthew 5:9 (NABRE)

Robert (Bob or Bobby) DeSilva (Brother)

When my father shared the history of our family, he told me an ancestor changed our surname from Silva to DeSilva. His dad was Mexican, and his mother's family was mostly Irish. I am the only boy and the eldest of four children born to my parents, Robert and JoAnn DeSilva. *Robert* seems to be a popular male name in our large family, so there are a bunch of Roberts, including my father, me, and my son. Dad is called Bob as a nickname. I'm called Bobby or Bob, and my son is called Bob or Bobby. My brother-in-law's name was Robert (Bob) and my nephew's name is Robert and he is called Rob. That's just an interesting tidbit about our family. We have a large extended family. It's great!

When I was a child, on the weekends when we didn't have activities to attend, our family would visit our grandparents or Uncle Tommy. We were always glad to visit our welcoming family members. I remember the many family barbeques our parents hosted in the backyard when we lived in Queens. Lots of our relatives attended those fun get-togethers. After Mom, Dad, Angela, and I moved from Queens to Long Island in 1973, we continued having family barbeques and cookouts. Our first house in Long Island was a three-bedroom ranch. We had one bathroom and a full basement. This meant along with my parents, I would have my own bedroom, and Angela would have one, too.

Our younger sister, JoAnna Rosalie DeSilva, was born in 1974, which was two days after my eleventh birthday. I guess you could say she was my birthday present that year – at least for me she was. We nicknamed her the *Long Island Baby*. For a while, she and Angela shared a bedroom. When we moved to our last family home on Long Island, we had four bedrooms. This time, Angela had earned her own bedroom sanctuary, so JoAnna and our baby sister, Annmarie, who was born five years after JoAnna, shared a room. Over time, our two siblings grew to be extremely close.

I'd like to think JoAnna and I had a lot in common, but no one was like her, not even my other two sisters, Angela or Annmarie. From the moment she was born, I always thought of my younger sister as being *special*. JoAnna never fought or argued with our sisters or me. There was never any sibling rivalry or wasted energy spent by yelling at anyone; instead, JoAnna's energy was used for her life-long passions of music and helping others. She was all heart. As the perfect kid for my parents, she always did her homework without being reminded and practiced the piano without being told. I wish I could say the same about me and my homework; the truth of the matter is I never did mine, but my younger sister was self-disciplined from birth. It was as if she never wanted to displease or be a burden to anyone.

From the time she could walk and talk, JoAnna enjoyed anything having to do with music. This included singing, dancing, playing the piano, and performing in plays. Those were the things she loved and filled her soul, and not only did she love them, my sister was good at them, too. I guess you might say she followed her heart and found her passions.

Our family enjoyed Christmases and holidays when the whole family from far and wide could come together. It was fun to have our grandparents, aunts, uncles, and cousins visit with us during the special times of the year, and my sisters and I enjoyed being together with just our parents, too. Because we lived in New York, it often snowed in the winter. We'd make snowmen, intent on our work until we gave birth to the *most perfect* snowman ever. And no afternoon was complete until we had a snowball fight. After becoming a parent myself years later, I'm sure our parents could hear lots of laughter, shrieks, and playful screams coming from outdoors and basked in their children's glee. I know as a parent I did. A child's laughter is a beautiful blessing to anyone's ears.

Afterwards, when we were tired, we'd lie on our backs in the powdery white and cold fluff to create snow angels. It was always fun to stand back and study our different formations before retreating into our inviting home to thaw out. The warmer months found us retreating to the backyard and playing typical kids' games: basketball, badminton, and croquet. Sometimes, we just sat together and talked.

Our proud parents were encouraging and supportive of anything we did. I especially remember they always made such a *big deal* over the school plays or church performances in which Angela and I had participated. It was always easy to locate their smiles among the other parents in the audience and wonderful to hear their litany of accolades on the way home. After JoAnna came along, even at a young age, it was obvious to the four of us that she was gifted and talented in music and performing. As she grew, her interests never waned. There was an increasing number of events and activities, like dance recitals, piano recitals, and school plays for our family to attend. We were always proud and delighted to watch our little sister perform; she put her heart and soul into everything she did. It was impossible not to smile and feel joyful to see her in the spotlight with her obvious passions betrayed by her beaming face. Sometimes, she seemed to glow in her delight.

There are times when I have regrets about the things I didn't do as a child and teenager. It seems those are the years that slipped by the fastest. It's almost as if I went to bed a boy and awoke the next morning as a man. Childhood and my experimental teen years were over; I was an adult. This meant society's normal expectations were to get a job, begin paying taxes, get married, buy a house, and have a family. I had grown up in the '70s and didn't go to college; instead, I got a job. I worked in the Department of Corrections at Riker's Island. Riker's is a whole city in itself and with all types of jails, some worser than others (minimum vs. maximum). I've had more jobs and cars than you can think of, but my favorite job was when I worked at the utility company.

As I reminisce now, I realize I always wanted to play the guitar, but I didn't pursue my interest. JoAnna wanted to play the piano, and she pursued her interest. The big difference is obvious: She took lessons and learned to play her chosen instrument, but I didn't. She worked hard to achieve her goals. As a consolation for my disappointment, I remind myself I did sing, which brings back favorite memories. I would sing one of my favorite songs, Billy Joel's "Piano Man," while JoAnna accompanied me on the piano. This was a special treat for our family.

The Piano Man
Sing us a song, you're the piano man
Sing us a song tonight
Well, we're all in the mood for a melody
And you've got us feelin' alright.

As my sisters and I aged through the years, we developed similar although different features, if that makes sense. I am six feet tall with light brown hair. Angela is five feet, five inches tall with jet black hair. JoAnna had dark brown hair that she dyed black and light skin; she was five feet, one inch tall. Annmarie is five feet, nine inches tall and has light brown hair. Dad and Mom are five feet, ten inches tall and five feet, seven inches tall, respectively. We were a unit of six, a close family who loved each other very much. There were times when we cheered each other on and times when we offered sturdy shoulders to catch the tears. Never in a million years could we have predicted or wanted to even imagine the possibilities of losing one member of our clan.

25

When JoAnna went away to Wagner College, we had the privilege of attending her Junior Recital on May 2, 1995, at the Performance Center, Campus Hall. The playbill read, "Wagner College Department of Performing and Visual Arts Presents JoAnna DeSilva soprano." I remember being so proud when I read my sister's name and bio.

> JoAnna DeSilva, the daughter of Robert and JoAnn DeSilva is a junior from Shirley, Long Island. JoAnna transferred to Wagner in the Fall of '94 from the College of Saint Rose in Albany. She is a vocal performance / education major and studies under the instruction of Sylvia Hummel.
>
> JoAnna has received a scholarship in academics and music from Wagner College. She has appeared in numerous musicals in high school and college and understudied the role of Peep-bo in the Wagner College production of *The Mikado*. JoAnna is a sister of Alpha Delta Pi Sorority and is a member of the chamber choir, opera workshop, Music Society, and has appeared as the soprano soloist for the Wagner College Choir. (Wagner College Department of Performing and Visual Arts)

Once again, we had the privilege of watching my sister perform for her Senior Recital on April 23, 1996, at the Music Performance Center, Campus Hall. The playbill read, "Wagner College Music department presents JoAnna DeSilva Soprano in her Senior Recital, Oksana Protenic, accompanist, with special guests: Bill Craane, bass, and Sean O'Hara, tenor." In addition to the bio they had used for her Junior Recital, they added the following paragraphs:

> JoAnna will graduate in December of 1996 with her Bachelors Degree in Music Performance / Education. JoAnna hopes to become an elementary music teacher

and to continue performing. (Wagner College Music Department).

There was a special note from JoAnna:

I would like to give special thanks to Sylvia Hummel, Oksana Protenic and Shirley Bock for all their help in making this performance possible. To the sisters of Alpha Delta Pi and Cheryl for supporting me through this ordeal and always believing in me, I love you all. (Thanks especially Jeanmarie, Cheryl, Jen, Daniella, Rachel and Monica because I am sure I drove you all crazy.) To all my friends and relatives for sharing this day with me and making it special. And finally, to my Mom and Dad, who are always there for me and whom I appreciate more than you will ever know, I love you both.

As JoAnna grew older, it seemed more and more people were drawn to her. My children affectionately called their aunt, *JoJo.* Mostly, I called her JoAnna. She led the children's choir at church, sang at Mass, taught music at school, directed plays for the kids to perform, and directed the chorus at school. Our family enjoyed attending as many school plays and performances, which JoAnna led or directed, as possible.

Her boyfriend, Billy, actually proposed to her at one of the school's concerts. He was dressed as Frosty the Snowman, so she wouldn't know he was inside the costume, and it would be a complete surprise. The whole family was there to see the play and to witness his proposal. Billy and I were just starting to get to know each other. JoAnna and Billy had dated several years before getting engaged and married, but I'd never hung out with them. After my divorce was over and Rosalie came into my life, we began planning to enjoy fun activities together as couples.

When the accident happened, as the eldest, I knew I needed to be the strong one for my parents and family to lean on throughout the whole ordeal. This entailed handling painful tasks and responsibilities, like locating a picture of her for the newspapers and funeral home. It was difficult to see her smiling face in the photos, knowing I'd never see it in person again. In addition, my parents relied on me to assist them in planning the funeral arrangements, something I wish I'd never had to do.

JoAnna's wake was astounding and something I couldn't have believed if I wasn't there to witness it myself. The city had to close the entire town and a main parkway because of the heavy traffic of hundreds journeying to the funeral home. I would estimate there were over two thousand people in attendance, wedging their cars wherever they could find a place to park. Some folks parked at the Dunkin' Donuts and other businesses on both sides of the streets and sidewalks – anywhere they could fit a car. Lots of the men in blue knew JoAnna from the elementary school where she had taught their children. There were many policemen who were there paying their respects, and there were other policemen in full dress and white gloves standing outside to assist the many visitors. To me, it was like JoAnna was the president. Obviously, my sister was loved by multitudes of people.

I'm not a church-going man, but I'm a believer in the Bible and what Jesus wants us to do, which is to try and live our lives as much like Him as possible. This tragic loss of my sister definitely tested my faith. During the funeral, I was sitting in the church sanctuary when suddenly, I felt an urgent need to grab the available Bible from the back of the pew in front of me. There was an overwhelming desire to read something comforting for my chaotic spirit and rid me of this terrible grief. The Bible opened to Luke, Chapter 24; I began reading.

> The Resurrection of Jesus. But at daybreak on the first day of the week they took the spices they had prepared and went to the tomb. They found the stone rolled away from the tomb; but when they entered, they did not find the body of the Lord Jesus. While they were puzzling over this, behold, two men in dazzling garments appeared to

them. They were terrified and bowed their faces to the ground. They said to them, "Why do you seek the living one among the dead? He is not here, but he has been raised. Remember what he said to you while he was still in Galilee, that the Son of Man must be handed over to sinners and be crucified, and rise on the third day." And they remembered his words. Then they returned from the tomb and announced all these things to the eleven and to all the others. The women were Mary Magdalene, Joanna, and Mary the mother of James; the others who accompanied them also told this to the apostles, but their story seemed like nonsense and they did not believe them.
But Peter got up and ran to the tomb, bent down, and saw the burial cloths alone; then he went home amazed at what had happened. (NABRE)

When I saw my sister's name in the Bible, I read it over and over again. Even though I'd heard these verses read before, I didn't remember ever noticing my sister's name. I believed these verses were divinely given to me that day as comfort. I was hungry to discover who Joanna was. In Luke 8, I read the following:

Galilean Women Follow Jesus. Afterward he journeyed from one town and village to another, preaching and proclaiming the good news of the kingdom of God. Accompanying him were the Twelve and some women who had been cured of evil spirits and infirmities, Mary, called Magdalene, from whom seven demons had gone out, Joanna, the wife of Herod's steward Chuza, Susanna, and many others who provided for them out of their resources. (NABRE)

I was in awe of God's goodness to me that day, and His gift

29

of comfort through the scriptures. I later learned Joanna is Saint Joanna the Myrrh-Bearer. God knew my heart was broken, and I couldn't find any peace, knowing my sister was dead and her murderer was somewhere out there enjoying his life. He had fled the accident's scene. What coward does this?

Summary

- Turn to God at all times and in times of trouble; He is always there.
- Try and live life as much as Jesus as possible.
- Be prepared for tragedies and losses to test your faith.
- Read the Bible, His Word, for truth and comfort.

"I never wanted to go away, and the hard part now is the leaving you all. I'm not afraid, but it seems as if I should be homesick for you even in heaven."

Louisa May Alcott, *Little Women*

As a Daughter,
She Made Us Proud

"Do not be conquered by evil but conquer evil with good."
Romans 12:21 (NABRE)

JoAnn DeSilva (Mother)

After JoAnna entered high school, she joined the theater club and oftentimes invited her friends in the club to come over to our house to harmonize and sing upstairs in her bedroom. They seemed to enjoy having a place outside of the school building to practice. Besides, Bob and I enjoyed hearing their songs being sung overhead.

One time I remember JoAnna had auditioned for the leading role in a high school play. Unfortunately, she wasn't selected for the part. So, she focused her energy on assisting with the preparation of the backgrounds and sets. Just being included as part of the production was all that seemed to matter to her. When she auditioned the next time for the lead role in the play about George M. Cohan, she was selected as the lead's understudy.

Naturally, as a protective mother, I felt offended she hadn't gotten the lead role. I couldn't hide my disappointment, so I asked her, "JoAnna, why are you the understudy and not the lead?" I knew she was talented and deserved the leading role. I even went so far as to encourage her to quit.

But my daughter replied, "Ma, I'm in the play. Please don't be upset." It didn't bother her that she was just the understudy.

I felt ashamed and replied, "Okay, JoAnna. You're right. I'm sorry." That was all I could say.

As fate would have it, the person in the lead role got sick, and

JoAnna had to perform the role. Instantly, she became the star of the play. She won the lead role in the next play, one that would make you "cry your eyes out." She was the character Ethel Levey, George Cohan's first wife. The play was absolutely beautiful. Then, JoAnna won the role of Lucy in *Charlie Brown*. She never tried to outdo anyone else. She recognized what she could do, and that is all that was acceptable to her. She cared about everyone's feelings and failed to understand how people could be mean to each other.

Once in a while, my eldest daughter, Angela, and I used to have the normal Mother / Daughter disagreements, which bothered JoAnna. She empathized with her sister and would say, "Mom. Don't do that. You have to try and understand Angela." That's the way JoAnna handled everything. She was a true peacemaker.

JoAnna started a children's choir at church with the desire for all children to have an opportunity to be a part and to feel important. In addition to being the cantor at Sunday Mass, she was now the choir director at the Sunday 9:30 a.m. children's Mass. When she first began leading the choir, her boyfriend at the time would accompany her and assist with the kids. When the children's choir performed at Christmas and other Christian holidays, all the kids would stand erect and smile as they sang. It was easy to see they were happy, interested, and excited about what they were doing. To the kids who couldn't sing well, JoAnna assigned parts where they could come to the podium and read a passage of some kind. Every child stood out and was a vital part of the performance. My daughter instilled values in them she had learned for herself:

It didn't matter whether you were performing the lead role or not; you were in it; you were a part.

That is what mattered. These are some of the amazing beliefs she had and passed on to other people.

When it was time for JoAnna to go away to college, her father and I were happy to pay for her education. It wasn't long after our daughter graduated from college that she got a full-time position, teaching music at Boyle Road Elementary School. Once she had a steady income, she surprised her father and me by gifting us with a cruise to celebrate our thirty-eighth wedding anniversary. After we boarded the ship and located our stateroom, we found a lovely cake waiting for us. The icing read, "Happy Anniversary." She had thought of everything. JoAnna didn't ask her siblings to share in the cost of our trip. She didn't say, "Bobby, help me," or "Angela, help me." This was something special she wanted to do all by herself as a way of thanking us for her college education. This is the kind, grateful, and generous person our daughter was.

Whatever our daughter did, we were always there to support her, and we always sat up front in the audience. After she finished singing during Mass, she would step off the altar, come to where her father and I were sitting, and kiss each of us. Then she'd return to the altar. It was important to her to have our approval. And no matter where JoAnna performed, Angela, her husband, Bob, their children, and Annmarie were always there with us to support her and enjoy the presentation.

As an elementary music teacher, JoAnna once encouraged a nine-year-old student to go to Gateway Playhouse, a premiere professional musical theater in Bellport, New York, to audition.

"You can do it. You're great! Go try out!" she pleaded while urging him to agree. As a result, the student accepted her encouragement and advice and was selected to perform in the *Phantom of the Opera*.

Our daughter took us to see the little boy perform in *Phantom of the Opera*. After the play was over, JoAnna was invited backstage to meet the actors, so we were thrilled to accompany her. As we made our way through the rows of actors to the young boy, the actors expressed disbelief at how young our daughter was and how she had been able to influence the young boy to audition for the play. One of the actresses wrote a kind note in our playbill,

34

acknowledging JoAnna for recommending the little boy.

JoAnna was constantly searching for and pursuing ways to ensure all of her students had an opportunity to feel important and to be important. That was a strong desire of hers. As a result of her dedication and popularity, the school's choral group grew from a small size to a large number of 150 singers. Here is a letter written to JoAnna on December 14, 1999, by Principal Patricia Bitcon, Boyle Road Elementary School:

Dear JoAnna,

Thank you for once again for putting on a terrific Winter Concert. The strings, band and chorus students were all well-prepared thanks to your hard work and enthusiasm.

Perhaps I am getting sentimental at this time in my career, but I thought this year's concert was the best ever. The kids and their parents certainly left here happy last night.

Thank you again for bringing music into our children's lives.
Sincerely,
Pat (Principal)

During one of the school's winter concerts, JoAnna was appropriately focused on her work -- playing the piano and conducting the chorus. Her future husband, Billy, had dressed like a snowman and walked out on the stage where she was. In front of the entire school, he got down on one knee and proposed marriage to her. You could see the different emotions registering on our daughter's face: confusion, shock, surprise, and joy. It was a beautiful, magical moment and a memory we'll never forget.

Here's another example of JoAnna's selflessness. After JoAnna had been dating her boyfriend for a few years and they were now engaged to be married, her younger sister, Annmarie, had met a nice young man and fell in love with him almost instantly. She was sure she wanted to be with him for life. So, Annmarie and her boyfriend, Jimmy, decided to get married as soon as possible.

This meant her marriage would occur before JoAnna's, which we had been planning for almost two years. Annmarie was worried that her desire to marry Jimmy as soon as possible would upset JoAnna. But when she asked her sister if it would be okay for her to marry first, JoAnna replied, "Sure. No problem."

JoAnna served as Annmarie's maid of honor, and five months later, Annmarie served as JoAnna's matron of honor. We held Annmarie's wedding at our home; the wedding we held for JoAnna was at the church. Both ceremonies were lovely and both daughters got the type of wedding they wanted. They were there for each other, and JoAnna was never upset about Annmarie's wedding happening first.

There was another selfless occurrence to happen. Our son, Bobby, wanted to propose to his girlfriend, Rosalie, and make it something special and memorable. So, he asked JoAnna if he could propose marriage to Rosalie at her wedding.

"Of course," JoAnna agreed.

Bobby followed through and proposed marriage to Rosalie at JoAnna's wedding, on what became a beautiful date with special memories. Our daughter was selfless and wanted everyone to be happy. She had a giving and loving heart.

Summary

- It's okay not to be the lead; be thankful to be a part.
- Try to understand the feelings and motives of others.
- Find ways to help others find their gifts and talents.
- Be encouraging and supportive of everyone.
- Show gratitude at all times.
- Allow others to have the spotlight, too.

"One of the sweet things about pain and sorrow is that they show us how well we are loved, how much kindness there is in the world, and how easily we can make others happy in the same way when they need help and sympathy."

Louisa May Alcott, *Jack and Jill*

As My Younger Sister, She Was Funny

"Do not rebuke an older man, but appeal to him as a father.
Treat younger men as brothers, older women as mothers,
and younger women as sisters with complete purity."
1 Timothy 5: 1-2 (NABRE)

Angela Rosalie DeSilva Zippel (Sister)

I am the second child born to Robert and JoAnn DeSilva. At birth, my given name was Angela Laurie DeSilva. After Confirmation, I took my maternal aunt Rosalie's name as my middle name – Angela Rosalie DeSilva – because she was my Confirmation Sponsor.

I remember when JoAnna was born in 1974; it was exciting to have a little sister. I don't remember ever being jealous of her or of having a new addition to the family. Even though I was seven years older than JoAnna, I enjoyed playing with her. We used to have these little Monchichi plush monkeys that we played with often. We had fun making them little beds out of shoe boxes. We'd decorate their beds and find pretty pieces of cloth for their bedding.

One day our mother was driving my brother, Bobby, a friend of his, JoAnna, and me, when all of a sudden, we turned around and discovered the back of the car was on fire. Mom quickly pulled over onto the shoulder of the road, and we all jumped out. I pulled JoAnna out of the backseat before the entire car went up in flames.

On another occasion, Mom was driving JoAnna and me to Modell's Department Store to shop for school clothes. I was around eleven or twelve, and my sister was four or five. Mom and I were sitting in the front seat, and JoAnna was sitting in the backseat, putting her Monchichi to bed in its shoe box. Out of nowhere, the car went up in flames. My mother and I jumped out. I ran to the back door and pulled JoAnna out of the car to safety. As a second thought, I also grabbed the shoebox with the toy monkey. It's hard to believe this happened twice on two different times and two different vehicles. I was relieved and happy I was able to pull my sister to safety both times.

My siblings and I were blessed with parents who had a great marriage. We were raised in a supportive, harmonious environment. Daddy worked long and hard hours for the City, and later, when my sisters were older, Mom worked part-time at the YMCA, teaching little kids how to swim. It's humorous that my brother and I still don't know how to swim, but Mom did teach both of my sons to swim.

I met my husband-to-be when a mutual friend visited our home, and he tagged along. It was love at first sight. I remember the date well – it was June 6 – JoAnna's birthday. Six months later, Bob (another Robert) and I had planned our wedding and were married in 1988. The dresses I chose for my bridesmaids were pink and a Southern Belle type. Thirteen-year-old JoAnna was one of my bridesmaids – a junior bridesmaid.

Bob and I have two sons and a daughter. Our eldest child is Robert Michael, and we call him Rob. He is thirty-two. Our second son's name is Brian, who is thirty. Our daughter is Samantha, who is now seventeen. At her baptism, JoAnna and Billy became her godparents. Aunt JoJo never showed any difference or bias in affections between her nephews or her nieces. For Samantha's Confirmation, she chose Daddy to be her Confirmation Sponsor. He was extremely touched by his granddaughter's choice and his distinction to stand with her.

We all were interested in music but not to the extent JoAnna was. Dad's mother also played the piano and sang. Our son, Brian, played the trumpet for a while. Samantha sang in the school chorus and played the clarinet. As a matter of fact, Brian has expressed a desire to learn how to play the piano. We have JoAnna's upright piano in our living room. My grandson is five years old; he often goes to her piano and plays. He has a gift, so we definitely want to give him piano lessons.

Samantha used to compete in little girl beauty pageants. JoAnna would accompany us to the pageants. It was lots of fun, and we'd always get our pictures taken. These competitions were one of the special things we did together. JoAnna's favorite character was Betty Boop. She even looked like Betty Boop with her dark hair dyed black, her red lipstick, and her alabaster skin. Based on the information I've read about this character, even their personalities were similar.

Prior to the tragedy happening the following January, Samantha had made it to the National Competition in June or July. We were all excited for her to compete, so JoAnna, Billy, my parents, my husband, Bob, and son, Brian, came with Samantha and me to the competition. Brian, who loves to take pictures, had close relationships with both Uncle Billy and Aunt JoAnna. Actually, the three of them were best friends who enjoyed a lot of activities together. While we were at the National Competition, we had some downtime in our schedule, so we decided to visit the Bronx Zoo.

Upon entering the butterfly exhibit, we all saw a lovely Monarch butterfly sitting on a vivid purple flower. JoAnna was staring at it, and she began whispering to Brian, "Take its picture. Take its picture. Make sure you get a close-up." Brian's resulting close-up was breathtaking. He had captured the loveliness of the butterfly's restful moment.

JoAnna was really into magazines. She loved to scan through their many pages and advertisements to find items she liked and wanted for her wedding. When she was a little girl, she'd begun planning for her Cinderella-like wedding day. It was going to be a big church wedding, and her dress was going to be the fluffiest white dress she could find.

Well, the years had flown by and suddenly she was planning (or putting on the final touches) her wedding and reception.

"Look, Angela! I want this! Look! Let's get this. I want that!" she'd say while we were planning her bridal showers and other events.

One day, I came home to find a page pulled from a magazine, hanging on my refrigerator. It seemed to be an article with a picture of pink bridesmaid dresses. As I got closer, I realized why the dresses looked so familiar and why the article was on my refrigerator where I couldn't miss it. The title of the article read, "The Worst Bridesmaids Dresses of the '80s." These were the same dresses my bridesmaids had worn. And I knew exactly who had hung it on my refrigerator. JoAnna was funny that way.

In the end, JoAnna had a big beautiful wedding in August – the one she'd always dreamed of having. Annmarie and I wore a greenish-colored dress, and the bridesmaids wore peach-colored dresses. One of the highlights of the wedding ceremony was when JoAnna sang "The Wedding Song," a popular song that was written in 1969 by Noel Paul Stookey of *Peter, Paul, and Mary*. I can still hear her beautiful soprano voice singing it.

Oh the marriage of your spirits here has caused Him
to remain For whenever two or more of you are
gathered in His name There is Love. There is Love.

Afterward, the newly-weds honeymooned in Hawaii.

Our son, Rob had a good friend, Bruce. They used to enjoy doing a lot of things together. As a result of their friendship, our two families became close to the point, I considered Bruce's mother, Roseanne, as one of my closest friends. In September, Bob and I were going out for the evening, and JoAnna was babysitting Samantha at her house. Brian was at a friend's home, and Rob was going to a football scrimmage game.

As Bob and I were dropping off Samantha, JoAnna told me, "Make sure you're home by 11:00. I'm not staying up all night."

"Okay. We will." I replied.

Unfortunately, on the way home, we saw flashing lights and an ambulance, which always makes me feel bad for the other party. Bob and I drove to JoAnna's house, got Samantha, and went home. Later we discovered that Bruce, his mother, Roseanne, and his sister were driving somewhere when a woman blew a red light and smashed into them. Roseanne and her daughter died in the accident. As a result, Bruce was left handicapped and confined to a wheelchair. He couldn't speak. Even today, he doesn't speak.

The entire month of January 2004 was bizarre. The first weird thing to happen was on January 4. We had a sweet little Maltese dog named Freddie. I let him out that Sunday morning to do his business and walked to the garage to wash the laundry. When I came out of the garage, Freddie was gone. I ran around the yard and into the house, searching for him. But I couldn't find Freddie anywhere. Anxiously, I jumped into my car and began driving, hoping to see him. Finally, I located him up the road. Someone had shot my dog! I placed Freddie in the car and drove home. Freddie was dead.

Of course, I was extremely upset, so I called my husband, "Bob! Someone shot Freddie! Someone shot my dog. He's dead!" Bob told me to call the police, so I did and an officer came to write a report. In the meantime, I'd called JoAnna and Billy, and they came immediately.

It seemed strange to me then and even now because she'd

normally have come and stayed for a while to comfort me but not stayed the entire day. I loved Freddie and was grieving over his loss. I was also in shock that anyone could be so low as to shoot my dog. On this day, JoAnna stayed close, sympathizing with me over Freddie. At one point, she told me, "We'll have to get some comfort food to lighten the atmosphere around here."

Bob's and my wedding anniversary is January 23. Our son, Rob, had a basketball game that night, so we invited JoAnna and Billy to attend it with us. After the game, we went to a restaurant for dinner. I remember Bob was in a really bad mood that night.

After a while, JoAnna looked at him and said, "You know, Bob? You just have to stop it. Life is really too short."

She was the kind of person who told you how it was. Who could have predicted that eight days later, my sister would pass away? That conversation stayed with my husband. JoAnna and Bob had always been close; she'd thought of him as a big brother, and he'd thought of her as a little sister, who he'd known for sixteen or seventeen years, ever since she was twelve or thirteen.

On January 30, Bob and I were going out for a birthday party. A friend of ours was celebrating his fortieth "Over the Hill" birthday. JoAnna and Billy were going to babysit Samantha at our house. We stayed out until 2:00 a.m. because my sister had not asked me to be home by 11:00, as she had done in the past. If she had, we would have been home by 11:00, but she never said it or called me after we left for the party to say it. This seemed weird at the time. On the way home that night, I even thought, *Why didn't JoAnna call me and remind me to be home early? I would have been home already.*

I used to borrow JoAnna's clothes. On that particular night, I had borrowed a pair of her favorite boots. As soon as we arrived home, she said, "Take off those boots. They are coming home with me."

JoAnna and Billy were going to get their wedding pictures the next day, so she left with the boots. Of course, no one could have imagined what was going to happen next.

After JoAnna and Billy left, Bob and I went to bed. At six o'clock the next morning, I answered the telephone. My heart dropped out of my chest when I heard my mother screaming my sister's name, "JoAnna! JoAnna!" repeatedly. That's how I found out the devastating news that my sister was gone.

There were different routes to drive from my home to their home. But the particular route they had chosen that night was done for the purpose of avoiding the intersection where Roseanne's accident had occurred. Since September, none of us liked to go that way and would take a different route to miss that particular area. The accident had happened sometime between 2:20 a.m. and 3:00 a.m. on, now, January 31, 2004.

I knew my husband, Bob, and I would have to be strong for my parents. I think of Dad as being a strong man, but I knew this would be difficult for him, and I knew he'd need to support our mother. Somehow, my strength came from within by realizing what I was doing was out of love for my sister. My husband and a friend performed what I would consider the hardest task: Bob went to the morgue to identify my sister. No one else could have handled that task, and we're so thankful he could.

I telephoned my Aunt Rosalie (Mom's sister) in Florida, and she came quickly to assist us and comfort my parents. In preparation for the wake, Aunt Rosalie and I were left to select JoAnna's clothes – a white sweater and skirt. While I was choosing pictures to display on the board at the funeral home, I came across Brian's picture of the butterfly, which by now, was symbolic to me because it reminded me of our trip to the Bronx Zoo that summer. She had loved seeing that butterfly, and she had loved the picture Brian took.

After JoAnna's death, wake, and funeral, I was assisting my parents in finding a grief counseling group they could attend. Of course, I had no idea where to send them, but I had heard of The Compassionate Friends. It is organized for those "hoping to find a purpose in a life that suddenly seems so empty. Whether your family has had a child die (at any age, from any cause) or you are trying to help those who have gone through this life altering experience, The Compassionate Friends exists to provide friendship, understanding, and hope to those going through the natural grieving process" (compassionatefriends.org). But I recognized at the time, my parents weren't emotionally ready to attend a support group.

During the following months, my parents and other family members continued to receive sympathy cards and memorial letters from lots of folks. I'd absent-mindedly placed one envelope in my pocketbook before opening it. Several weeks later, when I finally did open the card, I immediately turned to what the sender had handwritten. It was from a student's family who had lost a son. They wrote about attending a helpful support group called The Compassionate Friends. Without looking at the cover of the card, I made a mental note and stuffed the envelope back into my pocketbook.

On a different day, when I was reconsidering the support group for my parents, I remembered the card and pulled it out of my pocketbook. This time when I pulled it apart and saw the front of the card, I froze. I was staring at a picture of a Monarch butterfly sitting on a purple flower. It looked like the exact same picture from the butterfly exhibit at the Bronx Zoo. Was this a sign from JoAnna? I believed it was. So, without hesitation, I immediately telephoned The Compassionate Friends to find our local chapter. My parents and I attended several sessions with the group, and they helped us. This was just amazing!

My friend, Debbie, completed paperwork and set up a scholarship fund in JoAnna's name. I'm the one who administers it each year with the donations folks send. This entails managing the donations, reading the submitted essays, and selecting the awardee. The requirement to apply for the JoAnna DeSilva Berggren Scholarship is the person has to attend college to become a music teacher. Their essay topic is, "With your love of music, what could you do for kids?" At the award ceremony, there is a lovely write-up and picture of JoAnna, as a reminder of the beautiful lady for whom the scholarship is named.

Sometimes, I feel courageous enough to drive past the place where JoAnna's accident happened. Actually, I have to pray each time, or I wouldn't be able to summon the courage to go past there. Today was one of the days I'd prayed for courage because I'd planned to take that route home. When my parents decided to write this book about JoAnna, I was driving along and thinking about whom I could get to contact the author. When I was almost home and had reached the place of the accident, I received a text message at that exact instant. It was from Emily, one of JoAnna's former students, whom I'd never met. Emily had been thinking of JoAnna and was writing to request a picture of her. I thought, *Wow! This is crazy!*

I visit the cemetery often, bringing decorations to place on JoAnna's grave on holidays, her birthday, and at other times. It's comforting for me to visit her. Actually, Bob visited her grave more often than I did. That's where he felt the closest to JoAnna.

My family and I decided to make a memorial garden in our yard for JoAnna. We planted a tree and some pretty flowers. Then we decided a bench would be perfect for the garden. I was going out for lunch with a group of co-workers to celebrate someone's birthday on April 16. I remember the date because it is also my mother's birthday. Over lunch, I was telling one of my friends about creating the memorial garden with a tree and flowers and shared with her that we wanted to get a bench for the site.

When our group arrived at the restaurant, the hostess seated us at a larger table. Immediately, we noticed a magazine rack behind our table. *How odd?* I thought. *It seems weird to have a magazine rack in a restaurant. And to have it located right behind our table is strange.*

My friend, Evelyn, grabbed the first magazine she could reach and opened it. There on the page she'd opened was a picture of a cement memorial bench with an engraved saying: "If tears could build a stairway, and memories a lane, I'd walk right up to heaven, and bring you home again."

It was perfect and just what I wanted. Of course, I ordered it for my yard. It was weird because JoAnna was always looking through different magazines for things she liked and wanted. And somehow, an advertisement for exactly what I wanted had found a home on the page of a magazine, and a magazine rack had found a strange location in the restaurant behind our table.

I began working for the county in 1999, but after JoAnna passed in 2004, I needed to do something different. So, finally in 2006, I winded up changing jobs and working in child support for the county. Along with nine other people, I was hired for that area. After the managers assigned us to our desks / work areas, I noticed the lady sitting across from me. She was younger and from Hawaii. As we talked, I discovered she had moved to the mainland and attended college in Colorado. Afterward, she had ended up in Long Island. One day as several of us were discussing the people we knew where she lived, it was shocking to learn that she'd rented her apartment in Port Jefferson Station from Nicole, one of JoAnna's closest friends.

She said, "My landlord is your sister's good friend."

What is the old saying? *It's a small world.*

I'm now in a different job where there are a few ladies whose children had JoAnna as their music teacher. Their children went to school with Emily, the former student who contacted me for JoAnna's picture, and who has a chapter in this book.

Summary

- Sometimes, comfort food can help a stressful time.
- Life is too short; make the most of each minute.
- God speaks to us in many ways: His Word, our thoughts, events, or other people. Be open to whatever way He chooses.
- Pray for courage so you can help others when they need it most.
- Focus on other's and their needs; being selfless and giving is rewarding.
- Be open to miracles and divine interactions.

"Help one another is part of the religion of our sisterhood."

Louisa May Alcott

As My Protector,
She Reassured Me

"Be on your guard, stand firm in the faith,
be courageous, be strong."
1 Corinthians 16:13 (NABRE)

Annmarie (Sister)

JoAnna and I were born five years apart. My birthday is June 26, which is also Saint Anne's birthday, who is the Mother of Mary, our Blessed Mother. My maternal great-grandmother, Rosario, suggested my parents name me *Annmarie*. I was born on Saint Anne's birthday, so I should be named for her (Anne) and the Blessed Mother (Mary or Marie). Thus, I was named Annmarie. Because of JoAnna, my parents, and older siblings, I'm sure I was the spoiled baby of the family. You'll have to ask my parents or brother and sister for confirmation.

Strangely enough, JoAnna is a part of every memory I have. I was the closest person to her because she and I shared a bedroom, and she became my protector. Believe it or not, we never fought. She was the best sister anyone could ever have and someone who would do anything for anyone.

When I was young, JoAnna was very protective of me. As it turned out, after we grew up, she was only five feet, one inch tall or so -- small, smart, and sweet – and I was five feet, nine inches tall, so it was my turn to be protective of her.

We used to do lots of outdoor stuff together. One thing I remember is when I was five and she was ten, JoAnna made up this song, "We are Pals." We'd run down the stairs holding each other's arms. Then we'd skip and sing, "We are Pals." From that time until the day she died, whenever she sent me a card, she'd end it by writing, "We are Pals." I've kept all of those cards, but I don't look at them because they make me sad.

My sister was just as protective of me as before — if not more — when I began going to school. She was my big sister, and she already knew the ropes at school, so her job was to ensure I learned them — what to do, when to do it, where to go, and the like. She was very serious about her role as a big sister because I was her little sister.

JoAnna and I did everything together. Each year, our parents took us on a family vacation to the Poconos or to our favorite, Disney World, where we went many times. Aunt Rosalie, Uncle Sal, and their two sons, Frankie and Sal, always accompanied us on our vacations. Our cousin, Sal, was JoAnna's age. Frankie was older -- Angela's age.

My sister wasn't fond of heights, so whenever we drove over bridges, JoAnna would scrunch down in the car's floorboard where she couldn't see out of the window and stay there until we were safely on the other side of the bridge. I loved going over the bridges. Heights didn't bother me.

Once we'd arrive at Disney World, I'd head for Space Mountain, my favorite ride. I didn't want anyone but my sister to ride with me, which she reluctantly did even though she disliked heights. Thankfully, this roller coaster was in the dark, so she never knew when the hills and dips were coming. She just knew they were coming.

No matter where we were, but especially at Disney World, JoAnna liked to eat ice cream. Her favorite foods were Mexican and Greek dishes, so whenever we went to Disney World, visiting Epcot Center and all of its many countries was a must. Hands down, Mexico was our favorite country to visit. That's where we could eat the delicious food and buy maracas. The last time Mom, Dad, JoAnna, and I vacationed at Disney World and Epcot Center, I was sixteen and my sister was twenty-one. Anyway, we always had a blast!

Unfortunately, JoAnna nor I ever knew our paternal grandfather (Daddy's father) who died before we were born. Our paternal grandmother (Daddy's mother) became completely blind before JoAnna and I were born, so she never got to see what we looked like. We visited her every year in Mamaroneck, New York. We knew both of our maternal grandparents (Mom's parents), but our maternal grandfather died when I was eleven years old.

Some of my favorite memories are of Easters. When we were young, we got a new frilly Easter dress and patent leather shoes to wear to church on Easter Sunday. I always got to wear a bonnet. I loved my bonnet with the pink lace. But my favorite thing about Easter was getting to hear JoAnna sing. My sister had the most beautiful voice. She often sang me to sleep at night and continued doing so even when I was older. JoAnna had begun singing in church when she was ten years old, eventually becoming the cantor for Sunday Mass. Later, she started a children's choir at the church. She used her talents and skills to make other people's lives better.

JoAnna remained focused – she never wavered. She always did her homework and helped me complete mine. Because of our ages, we attended different schools but in the same district. Every year the high school put on a play; usually, my sister played the lead role. The elementary school would take the students to see the plays, so I'd get to see my sister. I was so proud of her.

I remember telling all of my friends, "That's my sister."

I felt lucky, too. At night, I'd get to see her perform again when my parents went to see the play. I could tell they enjoyed watching her sing, dance, act, and play the piano as much as I did. We were blessed by JoAnna.

Sadly, as the years passed, I dreaded turning twelve because it would mean JoAnna would be heading to college. I'd have to say goodbye to my big sister. I remember when the dreaded day arrived, and our parents were helping JoAnna pack the car with her things. That's when reality washed over me. She and I wouldn't be sharing a room anymore. She wouldn't be at the supper table with Mom and Dad and me as before. She and I wouldn't be watching *Friends, South Park,* and *Family Guy* together. JoAnna wouldn't be there to help me through middle school and high school. My whole life was changing. I was overwhelmed. Until this time in my life, I had been shielded, but this was the worst trauma I'd ever experienced. JoAnna was leaving me. But even so, my most vivid memories of that day are of my poor sister throwing up the entire trip to college because she was nervous about being away from home; she didn't want to leave us. I don't know why I wasn't throwing up beside her.

When JoAnna went away to college and left me, my whole life seriously changed for the worst. I turned bad. I stopped attending school. I started smoking pot. I stopped singing. My best friend was gone away for four years to college. Until she returned home in 1998, I was rebellious and sad. As a result, I never made my Confirmation when I was thirteen or fourteen years old.

Finally, my sister's four years of college were over, and JoAnna returned home. It was the summer of 1998, which became the most incredible summer of my life because she was finally home again! But I quickly realized she was different. I was shocked to learn she had gotten a little cherry tattoo on her hip. So, I asked her to take me for my first tattoo, and she did. I chose a bunch of flowers and vines. JoAnna chose a second tattoo – a big Betty Boop – which she placed on her leg. Her love for Betty Boop had come about the previous four years. She even looked like Betty Boop, lovely, small with porcelain skin, red lipstick, and dyed black hair.

Another surprise was learning that JoAnna had begun smoking cigarettes but not really because she didn't know how to smoke. She never inhaled. One day, I complained because I was tired of watching her waste good cigarettes. "Would you just stop? You're not really smoking." So, she did.

JoAnna had literally been an angel all of her life. She had never been the type of girl to get tattoos and smoke cigarettes. Even though college had opened new doors for her, she remained the angel I always knew. One door that had been opened during college was she had fallen in love. She'd met the young man whom she would eventually marry – Billy – who was into Harleys and tattoos. Apparently, he'd had a big influence on her.

JoAnna and I hung outside in the backyard every day that summer. We'd laugh about my memories of bringing beers to our great-grandmother in the backyard when she was ninety-six. I always sneaked and sipped the foam before I handed over the beers. She lived a long life of 102 years. Maybe it was the beer that did it.

When we were tired of the backyard, we'd drive around, listening to music blaring from the radio and singing. My sister was a singer and hearing her voice was my favorite thing. I still have videos and tapes of her, but even now, I can't bring myself to watch or listen to them. We listened to pop and classical music. My favorite song she sang was "Ava Maria." To this day, I can't hear that song because it breaks me into pieces because I can still hear her singing. It was beautiful.

Before either of us married, JoAnna planned a trip to Las Vegas and wanted me to go with her. Although I am afraid to fly, I decided to go. I remember saying these words: "If anything happened to you, I'd die anyway." This was two years before she did die.

I hated Vegas. It was the worst place even though we were staying at Bally's Hotel and Casino. Now, of course, I'm glad I went with her. We didn't play at any of the cards, chips, or spin-the-wheel tables. But until I'd experienced Las Vegas and quickly lost my money, I didn't know how much I disliked gambling. I found myself wondering, *What am I doing here?* JoAnna, on the other hand, enjoyed playing the slot machines. While we were there, we went to the "Howie Mandel Show," which was hysterical. We also went to the Stratosphere Tower where my sister, who had always been timid and scared of heights, literally shocked me by riding the X-Scream at the top of the tower. I wouldn't go on it with her, and she didn't insist. It was extremely scary. Somehow, we had switched our individual perceptions of fear.

JoAnna's and my taste in clothes were the same as we grew older. In the '90s, I remember having a pair of shiny satin pants that I loved to wear. Before she got married, JoAnna followed the Weight Watchers diet and lost about twenty-five pounds, so my pants finally fit her. I happily gave them to her because I had gained weight and couldn't wear them any longer. I was never jealous of JoAnna, but I have to admit, she looked beautiful wearing those pants. That may sound hard to believe, but it's true – I was never jealous of my sister. Our relationship was never like that. It was based on love and being there for each other.

JoAnna was the girl who had dreamed of being the princess bride with the big church wedding and the beautiful white dress. I never wanted anything like that. Mom and my sister had been planning her wedding for six months when I met Jimmy, a musician and construction worker. I instantly knew this guitar-playing man was the right one for me, so I brought Jimmy home a week later to meet my parents and JoAnna.

Angela's son, my nephew, Rob, was going to be confirmed that weekend and had previously asked me to stand up for him as his Confirmation Sponsor. In order for me to make this commitment, I had to first be confirmed since I hadn't been when I was thirteen or fourteen. So, at the age of twenty-one, I asked JoAnna to stand up for me, and she did. I always chose her for anything. When someone is your Confirmation Sponsor, you take his / her name as your middle name. So, my nephew's name is now Robert Annmarie. My given name was Annmarie Linda DeSilva, but my name now is Annmarie JoAnna.

I told my sister, Angela, that Jimmy would be coming with me to the Confirmation and could play the guitar while JoAnna sang at the ceremony. Of course, I didn't realize he got nervous when he played in front of an audience. I had put him on the spot. After all, he was going to meet everyone in my family at the ceremony, which I imagine was nerve-wracking in itself. Fortunately, there was an instant connection between Jimmy and JoAnna because of their music. In addition, Jimmy is a really funny guy and made her laugh.

She told me, "He has a beautiful voice." For me, coming from her, it was the highest compliment he could receive, so I told him, "My sister thinks you sing really well." From that weekend forward, JoAnna and Jimmy enjoyed singing together for the family, which was always a treat.

A week later, Jimmy and I got tattoos of each other's names. We knew we wanted to get married soon, but I worried JoAnna might be upset with me if I wanted to marry before her. After all, she had been planning her wedding for a long time, but I should have known better. She wasn't in the least bit upset; she was happy for me and served as my maid of honor when we were married six months from the day we had met. Five months after that, I had the privilege of serving as a matron of honor in her wedding.

JoAnna and Billy were together for two years before they were officially engaged. One night when JoAnna's music students were giving a winter concert, our parents and siblings feigned interest in attending. My husband, Jimmy, had gone to the school earlier to play his guitar for the kids in JoAnna's classes. That made it seem only normal that we would want to attend. Besides, Jimmy did want to see the kids perform.

Of course, we secretly knew Billy planned to propose that night during the concert. As JoAnna was playing the piano and directing the chorus, he came onstage dressed in a snowman's costume. Poor JoAnna appeared confused; she had no idea who he was until he walked to her, removed his head, lowered himself onto one knee, and proposed. What a unique and sweet proposal! Her face showed a myriad of emotions: confusion, surprise, shock, delight, love, and extreme joy!

Jimmy had written a song for me that JoAnna sang during her wedding reception. The blending of the words, melody, and her voice created the most beautiful song I've ever heard. She sang harmony with Jimmy, and they recorded the song on her wedding CD. Everyone who attended the wedding received a copy of the CD as a favor.

De-Silva -- Berggren

> JoAnna DeSilva and William Berggren Jr. were married Aug. 2 at St. Jude Church in Mastic Beach. She is a music teacher for the Comsewogue School District and is the daughter of Robert and JoAnn DeSilva of Shirley. The bridegroom is a truck driver for FRP Sheetmetal in Bay Shore and is the son of William and Sophie Berggren of West Islip. The bride received a master's degree from Stony Brook University. The bridegroom graduated from West Islip High School. The reception was held at Majestic Gardens in Rocky Point. They live in Shirley. (Gein)

Jimmy and I moved to Winding River, about twenty minutes from my parents' home in Shirley. JoAnna and Billy lived in Mom and Dad's full basement. The newly-weds had planned to build a big home, along with our parents. This way, JoAnna would never leave them. Not only had my sister been protective of me, she was extremely protective of our parents. Among the four siblings, there was never any animosity.

On the night of the accident, we received a phone call at three o'clock in the morning. Jimmy woke me and calmly said, "We have to go to the hospital. Billy and JoAnna were in a car accident."

"What?" I almost shouted in alarm.

"JoAnna is in Brookhaven, and Billy is in Stonybrook."

Of the two hospitals, Stonybrook was more of a trauma center. I assumed JoAnna was going to be fine, and Billy was in worse condition. We drove in silence and arrived at the hospital the same time Angela and her husband arrived. I discovered later they had known everything, but we didn't. We walked inside and found my parents crying. Dad was hitting the walls with his fist.

A nurse came into the room and calmly told me, "Your sister expired."

I'll never forgot those empty words. I thought, *What? Was she a carton of milk?* There was no emotion, no sympathy or empathy in her monotoned calm voice. It was horrific.

I just cried and slipped to the floor.

Dad later suggested I read *The Five People We Meet in Heaven* by bestselling author, Mitch Albom. I read it. There is actually a line in there that says, "The nurse came and told me she expired like a carton of milk." I thought, *Oh, my God!*

As I recall that night, arriving at the hospital the exact time my sister and brother-in-law did was unreal. We were coming from two different directions and places. I believe everything has a meaning and / or a sign. The nurses yelled at my father for hitting the walls. Our treatment that night was horrible. They talked about my sister's death like it was nothing. I'll never go to that hospital again.

Mother wasn't there mentally or emotionally; she was in shock and just fell apart. My husband Jimmy took JoAnna's death hard when it happened. He was angry, but he focused his attention on me. He tried to be there for me. Her death was hard then, and it is hard now.

My sister's wake is a blur with hundreds of faceless people attending. Our family had a police escort that night because the main highway had been closed due to the heavy traffic of people coming to the funeral home. Obviously, as you can imagine, my mother fell apart. I am very close to my mother and talk to her twice a day. It hurt me to see her so broken. At the time, I actually prayed God would take her. I couldn't stand to see her in that condition.

At the wake, I had planned not to go inside to see JoAnna, but someone convinced me to go in by saying, "You might regret it later if you don't." I wish I'd never listened to that person. I wish I'd never gone in. I wish I'd never seen her because it wasn't her. I diverted my eyes to her hands. When I was a kid, I always admired JoAnna's beautiful hands and polished nails as she played the piano. They looked the same – the only things that did. I left, sorry I went in there and relieved my mother never did.

After the wake that night, we returned to my parents' home. Mom was sitting at the kitchen table. Everyone encircled her because we all recognized how she was falling apart. She hadn't been okay since the night JoAnna died. My husband and I felt the need to escape for a few minutes. As we walked outside into the backyard, we looked up at the sky. There was a huge halo over the house. It wasn't over any other house – just my parents' home. I'm not insane because Jimmy saw it as well. Excitedly, I rushed inside to tell Mom. That's when I heard Mom calling my name. Mom's voice seemed different. It had totally changed; she sounded like my mother again.

She was smiling. "JoAnna just came to me and told me everything was going to be okay. I felt her."

JoAnna's comfort had come the exact moment the halo was situated over the house. Over the years, there have been lots of signs, but we could actually see the physical change in our mother's face, demeanor, and voice. At this point, she also knew she was going to be okay. When Jimmy and I arrived home that night, the halo was over our house, too, and no one else's. My sister was comforting us, too.

I didn't go to the cemetery, and I've never been since. As a Catholic, I understand why people are buried. But I'm afraid if I go to visit her grave, I will only think of her being in the ground. My sister, Angela, and her family go many times during the year – for her birthday, Christmas, Easter, and other special dates. Angela enjoys bringing JoAnna flowers. I can't do that. I have no idea if my brother, Robert, has ever been.

After the man who killed my sister was apprehended, I didn't go to the trial. Angela, her husband, Bob, Dad, and my brother, Bobby, went. I stayed with my mom. Our maternal grandmother, Angelina, who was in a nursing home with probable dementia, never knew JoAnna had died. Mom never told her. Thankfully, Grandmother Angelina never asked Mom where JoAnna was during Mom's daily visits to see her. It was difficult for Mom to hold it together in her mother's presence, but somehow, she did. I'm told that one day, Grandmother Angelina told Mom that her daughter (JoAnna) had been visiting her every day.

Our family received two sets of letters. We received letters from family, friends, and even JoAnna's teenage ex-boyfriends. The outpouring of sympathy, support, and love were amazing. Everybody said my sister was incredible and called her an angel. This is true. JoAnna was an angel all of her life. She used her talents and skills to make other people's lives better.

JoAnna was like the glue who held our family together. JoAnna's death really tore us apart. Sixteen years later, everything in my life is different now. At one time, I didn't see my brother for a year, and I missed him. There are stupid things people fight over that don't really matter. We, of all people, should know. My husband convinced me to go see my brother, and I'm glad I did. That's not the way we were raised. We realized we had had a stupid misunderstanding; now we're trying to reconcile.

Our parents no longer live in New York; they live in Florida, where they wouldn't be if JoAnna were still here. They weren't the people who were ever planning to move away from their home and their roots. It's tough because we miss them.

JoAnna used to make a bunch of Weight Watcher foods, and she'd make this Mexican rice dish with chicken all the time. It was delicious! Actually, I had some she had given to me before she died. I froze it and kept it in my freezer for four years because I'm crazy. It was never out of my sight that way. Finally, my husband talked me into throwing it out, but I still kept the Tupperware bowl it was in.

Everyone recognized JoAnna as the rock in our family. She was like an angel, never getting into drugs or having other vices. Throughout her entire life, she was always close to God and enjoyed working in the church. My sister was sweet, loving, giving, talented, and the best singer I've ever heard.

I used to say, "I don't know where she came from. I believe she must have come from Heaven."

The old cliché is "hind sight is twenty-twenty," and I agree. I believe it was meant for me to find and marry Jimmy as quickly as I did because without him, I couldn't have survived losing my sister a year later. It was meant for him to be there for me when JoAnna was gone.

There are times when Jimmy starts to play the song he wrote for me, "After the Fall," but I have to leave the room. It's not that I want to hurt him; it's not that I don't want to hear the song. It's just all I hear is her voice singing it, and the emptiness still hurts.

Summary

- Use your talents and skills to make other people's lives better.
- Don't argue with family and friends. But if you do, make-up. Life is too short to stay apart.
- Everything has a meaning or a sign. Remain aware.
- Follow your instincts; don't allow others to convince you of something you don't want to do. To your own self be true.

"Painful as it may be, a significant emotional event can be the catalyst for choosing a direction that serves us - and those around us - more effectively. Look for the learning."

Louisa May Alcott

As My Sister-in-Law, She was a Cool Chick

"For God did not appoint us to suffer wrath but to receive salvation through our LORD Jesus Christ. He died for us so that, whether we are awake or asleep, we may live together with him. Therefore encourage one another and build each other up, just as in fact you are doing."
1 Thessalonians 5: 9-11 (NIV)

Jimmy (Brother-in-Law)

I wrote After the Fall for my wife. That song poured out of me, taking a total of ten minutes to write. Songs like that are very few and far between. I can write music all the time, but I'm my worst critic. I have difficulty being able to stop writing, editing, and revising.

I was a guitar player, playing in some bands, plus I was a cabinet maker. One of my buddies said, "Hey, there is this girl. She's really cool, and her name is Annmarie. I want you to meet her."

So, Annmarie and a friend came to Club Blue, a bar in Rocky Point, New York. I had arrived early to set up my gear properly. Then I knew I could leave it and walk away. I saw this girl sitting there with her friend and thought, *Wow! There's no way that could be her. Mark would know this gorgeous girl wouldn't be interested in me*. But just in case, I set up my rig and threw the guitar strap over my head, joking around with the base player. I played a little guitar and received a rousing applause. That's when Mark introduced me to her.

We hit it off great. A piece of her shirt had broken, so I ran back to the dressing room and put on a sweaty shirt. I returned and gave her the dry shirt to wear. She went to the bathroom and put the shirt on. I wore the sweaty shirt while we performed. I was just being my normal self. I'm no monetary wizard or brain, but I am a gentleman. I didn't realize Annmarie was thinking, *I'll never hear from him again*. Annmarie supposedly was *done* with guys; she hated them and thought most were scumbags. The next day I called her, and six months from the day we met, we were married. That's a quick overview.

Two weeks after meeting Annmarie, I asked her if she wanted to take a ride with me to the guitar center in Commack because I wanted to look at some equipment. We both went to get tattoos together. I had *Annmarie* tattooed on my wrist, and she had *Jimmy's Princess* tattoed on her wrist. I had gotten a tattoo on my other wrist, too.

When we arrived at the guitar store, three of my friends just happened to be there. They were looking a little funny, so it finally dawned on me. Here I was with both of my wrists bandaged, and my girlfriend had her wrist bandaged. It looked like we had a suicide pact. "We just got tattoos," I explained.

I came to her house to meet the parents, and JoAnna was there. She was a beautiful girl. She was a little skeptical because Annmarie had talked me up so much about my playing the guitar well. I think she thought I could strum a few chords at best or could play lead guitar but couldn't play a song. I met Annmarie's parents, who were very nice.

So, we left to go to this family picnic. This is the same weekend I was to meet her entire family. Annmarie threw me out in front of her family and said, "This is my boyfriend. He's going to play the guitar for you."

I had nothing prepared, so I just winged it. I pretended I was home in my bedroom, strumming acoustic. I sang a bunch of Eric Clapton, Neil Young, and stuff like that.

JoAnna came to me and said, "I'm impressed." She also

thought there was some nice guitar work going on, too, not just chords strumming along. She told Annmarie, "He can really play."

I told Annmarie, "I don't know if your sister likes me because she loves you. She works for everything she has. Nothing comes easy. I was impressed."

When JoAnna was going to record my song, After the Fall, I wanted us to sing it together. She had the perfect voice. You expect someone from college who sings at the Met to properly enunciate and hit everything at perfect pitch. But it doesn't work for rock- n-roll.

I was trying to get her to sing a song that was more laid back. I told her several times, "You're going to have to dumb up your vocal a little for me." She looked quizzical.

I explained, "Janice Joplin didn't sing like an opera star."

I wanted a beautiful girl's voice with me. And I wanted her, but I didn't want opera. I loved JoAnna's voice and wanted JoJo. So, she dumbed it up for me. She knew exactly what I meant. The next performance was perfect. It was easy – just one take. I sang **After the Fall** at her wedding, and we sang it together at the reception. She sang the "Wedding Song" at her wedding, and I accompanied her on the guitar.

JoAnna was an odd person because she was very smart – way smarter than I will ever be, but I do well with common sense. Then she married Billy, and I love Billy. God bless him, but he wasn't exactly valedictorian and not the type of guy who had the common sense stuff that comes to people naturally. He wasn't an idiot by any means – he did his job well – and we had good conversations – lots of fun – but he was a man who was into "Sponge Bob." I was always wondering, *Why?* It clicked for me one day.

Annmarie and I decided to celebrate our anniversary and drive upstate to the falls where we got married. We were going to stay in the same hotel and look at the falls. It was going to be nice. Ten minutes into the conversation, JoJo had invited herself and her mother and father to come along.

By the time the car came to get us, it was loaded down. I had maybe a two-feet space to fit in. It was supposed to have been Annmarie and me. But now after all is said and done, I thank God every day when I remember that we all went away together. We had a great time and a lot of laughs.

On the way to the falls, there was a sign we saw ahead. JoAnna was sitting up front in the passenger's seat. We were in the third row of this caravan.

JoAnna says, "There is a sign that says to go left. No. No. It says to go right. It says 'Left Albany.'"

I said, "We're not going to Albany; we're going to the falls. No. No. No. That's not what the sign says. The sign says 'Right unless to Albany.'"

So, JoAnna didn't listen to me. We drove two hours out of our way to find out we were on the wrong road and had to double back. She looked at me and said, "I'm sorry," in a sweet, meek little voice, like she didn't want to say she was sorry.

"Don't worry about it." After another couple of hours, we were almost there.

Then JoAnna said, "Look! There's our hotel."

I said, "No, JoJo. That's not our hotel. Ours is the one closer to the falls. We have a better hotel."

She said, "No that's it; I saw the picture."

I said, "JoJo, I think you looked at the wrong picture. That's the Hard Rock."

She didn't believe me. "You're wrong."

So, we got to the crossing at Customs, where we had to pay the toll.

She asked the guy, "What is that hotel over there?"

The guy said, "Oh. That's the Hard Rock."

It upset her that it wasn't the correct hotel because it meant I was right again.

She turned and said, "Jimmy, I'm sorry. I'll just have to be honest with you. I was just banking on the idea you were wrong because I had no idea. I just wanted to be wrong once," she said.

Another time, we were at J.R.'s Steak House. JoAnna announced they were going to have drinks. "How do they get that melon taste into this drink?"

I said, "They use a melon liqueur called Medori. It's light green. That's how they get the taste in there."

She said, "No way! They must use the real fruit. You can't get flavor like that in a bottle." So, she asked the waiter, "How do they get the melon taste in this drink?"

He said, "We use a liqueur called Medori."

JoAnna started laughing and cracking up. Finally, she said, "Jimmy, that will be the last time I try to prove you wrong." It was hilarious. She was a rip.

JoAnna invited me to come to her classroom. "Jimmy, could you come to the school? My students love to learn about music and are interested in the guitar, especially."

That was fine with me, so I went to the elementary school with a little amp, guitars, and effect pedals. The kids loved that. I allowed them to look at the guitars and play them. I could make an echo happen, or I could make the guitar sound like two different guitars. They loved that. I stayed for two hours and talked about guitars the entire time. The kids would look at JoJo before they asked a question. She was right on top of everything.

Billy's mother would still have been alone in a room, saying nothing. But JoAnna got her help; she responded and progressed to the point where we all could sit with her and carry on an interesting conversation. After JoAnna passed, sadly, we discovered a year later that his mother was back in her room and no longer talking. All of her attained progress was over.

JoAnna was a *go getter*. I wish I had a tenth of her *get up and go*. I'd be much better off. I was hoping as the years went by, some of that would rub off on me. I knew she was intelligent (my wife is intelligent, too), and I could talk to her about an array of subjects. JoAnna just understood me.

Another time I went to the school and played guitar along with Joanna for a concert her kids had at the Boyle Road Elementary School. I would never have had that touch with kids unless I had known JoAnna. I was learning a whole new level of patience. She helped me to grow, too, by injecting herself. She was a cool chick.

As far as looks, I think JoAnna favored her dad. Mrs. DeSilva was a knock-out in her own wedding pictures. I think JoAnna's eyes look like her mother's eyes. As adults, JoAnna and Angela looked like sisters; Annmarie doesn't look like them. When they were kids, the three girls looked a lot alike. All four of the siblings, have their dad's jaw. I guess you could say JoAnna was a good representation of both parents.

I didn't want to wait to get married. JoAnna's wedding wasn't coming off for a year. Why should we wait? We wanted to be together; we should be together. Everyone agreed, and it worked out where we could marry before JoAnna. Five to six months later, she had worked hard to lose weight and was a gorgeous bride.

Annmarie and I have been married seventeen years now. Most people we knew back then are divorced now. We're fortunate. Sometimes, I think about how life would be different if JoAnna were alive today. I know she and Billy would still be together. I imagine they would have three or four children. I think JoAnna would want a boy first and then a girl, another boy, and finally, a little girl. Billy would be a smarter person by now, ha ha. JoAnna still would be teaching music, and she might even have a spot on some off-Broadway musical. She still would be entertaining, the bright light in the room. She would be going to casting calls and trying out for roles. Knowing how she could sing and act, I think we'd see her performing periodically. We once told her she should be using her talents and art – not just focusing on other's art.

I would like to be an actor and trying out for parts. I considered going to Theater 3 in Port Jefferson Station to see if they needed a carpenter for their sets, so I could be around people who act. Maybe I could learn something. I know JoAnna would have gone in that direction because I know she could do it.

When I think of JoJo, I can't imagine what would have happened if I hadn't been here for Annmarie. JoAnna was Annmarie's rock until I came into the picture. Once when we were in Mamaroneck, New York, because Bob had a death in his family, somebody made a remark that could have escalated into a fight. I jumped in, made a joke, and everybody laughed before walking away.

JoAnna came to me and said, "It's nice to have someone intelligent around who can talk their way out of a fight instead of just jumping into one."

"Oh yeah? I can talk my way out of anything I do," I responded.

If JoAnna knew about this book being written about her, I think at first she would love the idea because she was content with herself. She gave you the air of a girly-girl and then wore pigtails around the house. She was self-confident. But even so, she'd ask, "Who would want to read a book about me?" She had that modest side.

Some people enjoy going around at parties and having fun, letting everyone know they are there. Others want to chill out first before coming out. JoAnna was the first type, and we miss her.

Lower yourself down to me, take me in your arms, never leave me. Think of what the future brings; thoughts of you and a little one could bring a tear to me. Lower yourself down to me, take me in your arms, never leave me. Never leave me.

-- From After the Fall by Jimmy Marchisotto

Summary

- Believe in yourself.
- Follow your passions and dreams.
- Try to adopt a *get up and go* attitude.

As a Sister-In-Law, She was Selfless

"God indeed is my salvation; I am confident and unafraid for the
Lord is my strength and my might,
and he has been my salvation."
Isaiah 12:2 (NABRE)

Rosalie DeSilva (Sister-in- Law)

My family owned an ice cream store in Shirley. The first time I
ever saw JoAnna was when she and Annmarie came in for ice
cream one day, and they continued coming in to get ice cream as
they apparently enjoyed the delicious treat. When I began dating
Robert DeSilva, their brother, he introduced me to them.

"My God! I remember you," I said. "You used to come to our
store for ice cream."

I thought JoAnna was amazing – like no other person I'd
ever met. Whenever she entered a room, everything seemed to
brighten up. Her positivity and optimism followed her. She was
the most selfless person I've ever known. I believe this because
of her many acts of generosity I witnessed during the time I knew
her but especially so because of the unique gift she gave to her
brother and me.

When Robert and I met, we were both divorcees with
children. My two boys, John and Antonio, were young. My little
guy, Antonio, was only eighteen months old when I introduced
Robert to my sons. Even though we'd both been hurt by the failure
of our first marriages and didn't want to get hurt again by rushing
into another relationship, we fell in love. Robert spoke with his
family about his intentions to propose to me, only he wasn't sure

how or when to do it.

That's when JoAnna said, "Propose to her at my wedding!"

Extremely grateful and somewhat relieved, Robert said, "That's a great idea, JoAnna! That's when I'll do it." How many people do you know who would offer such an altruistic opportunity to her brother?

We were at Robert's parents one day when JoAnna asked, "Rosalie, what is your favorite song?" I had no idea why she wanted to know, but I told her. Later I learned the reason at her wedding. Then she asked me if I would be one of her bridesmaids. I was surprised she'd want me in the wedding because Robert and I were just dating. We weren't engaged yet. But when she assured me this was what she wanted and extended the invitation again, I accepted. When she asked if John and Antonio could be a groomsman and a ring bearer, respectively, I was amazed and extremely touched. My boys mean the world to me, and their inclusion in this family event did, too. JoAnna always made everyone feel welcomed.

The wedding was a fairytale affair, and JoAnna was gorgeous in her beautiful princess-like wedding dress. During the wedding ceremony, JoAnna and her new brother-in-law, Annemarie's husband, Jimmy, sang two beautiful songs together while he played the guitar. They had recorded several songs on a CD (compact disc) that was given to all attendees as their wedding favor. Included on the CD was my favorite song. I almost wanted to cry. I realized why she'd asked me about my favorite song. But my surprises weren't over yet. I was speechless when Robert proposed marriage to me at her wedding. After I finally found my voice and said, "Yes," I noticed she was beaming with happiness – for Billy and her and for us. *What an amazing, selfless person she is,* I thought. *Who does this? The answer is easy. No one I've ever known but JoAnna.*

JoAnna was good at what she did. We enjoyed going to church and hearing her sing lovely solos. She also led the children's choir during church service every Sunday. It was interesting to watch the kids with her as she instructed them on how to sing, while accompanying them on the piano. JoAnna did it all. She was just — just amazing! There is no other word to describe her.

I have the honor of caring for my father, so after her wedding and Robert's proposal, Dad and I wanted to invite the family over for dinner. They graciously accepted our invitation, and everyone came to my home — my in-laws-to-be, Bob and JoAnn, JoAnna and Billy, Angela and Bob, Annmarie and Jimmy, and all the nieces and nephews. We enjoyed a nice dinner, lots of conversation, and playing cards. It was going to be a memorable evening.

That's when JoAnna said, "Oh, let's have an engagement party!"

My mother had died at an early age when she was twenty-nine, so I explained to JoAnna that I was experiencing a hard time, not having my mother here with us to celebrate my engagement.

"Rosalie," she began, "your mother wanted this for you. Your mother would be happy."

Yes, it was a memorable night.

I'll never forget the last Christmas with JoAnna. It was Christmas of 2003. Robert and I were going to be married, and Antonio was five years old. It was fun to watch him tear open JoAnna's gift in front of all the older cousins. They were saying, "Oh, my God! Oh, my God!" so it had to be something special. It was a popular video game. Antonio is twenty years old now, and he still has that video game.

On the night the accident happened, my father, sons, and I were asleep. The telephone rang. When I answered, a voice on the other end asked, "Is this Rosalie?"

"Yes. Who is this?" I asked. It was almost 3:00 a.m. "Who is this?"

"I'm calling from the hospital. May I speak to JoAnna?"

"What? JoAnna is home sleeping."

"There has been an accident."

"Well, she's not here. My sister-in-law doesn't go out at three o'clock in the morning. She is home sleeping." I couldn't understand who this was and why this person was calling.

"She was in an accident with her husband."

I knew I had to call Robert to let him know. I hated myself for having to tell him.

Like my mother, JoAnna was only twenty-nine years old when she passed. During the time I knew JoAnna, I never saw her get angry or cry. But this I do know. She is an angel. I know she is. She was a special person – amazing and very unique. We all knew she was absolutely special. She was good, generous, loving, and nonjudgmental. I never heard her judge anyone. Instead she accepted everyone.

After the accident happened, my father said to me, "I'm so upset. I only met JoAnna a couple of times, but she left a strong impression on me."

JoAnna connected with everybody. I think she was different from others at birth. I believe she was anointed by God for the purpose of using her life to bring people together – children, family, friends, and others -- whoever crossed her path. It was amazing to see how many peoples' lives she had touched. Not many people live that type of life.

I still have my CD JoAnna made as her wedding favor. I listen to it on the car's compact disc player whenever my husband isn't around because I don't want to upset him. We still talk about his sister every single day. I feel blessed and honored to have known the beautiful JoAnna.

Summary

- Strive to become generous, good, loving, and nonjudgmental.
- Include everyone; never exclude anyone.
- Focus on ways to make others happy by becoming selfless.
- See every occasion you spend with family and friends as a blessing.
- Life is not complacent; life is ever-changing.
- Live your life as an amazing example for others.

The Righteous Israelite

Lord, who may abide in your tent?
who may dwell on your holy mountain?
whoever walks without blame,
doing what is right,
speaking truth from the heart;
who does not slander with his tongue,
does no harm to a friend,
never defames a neighbor;
who disdains the wicked,
but honors those who fear the lord;
who keeps an oath despite the cost,
lends no money at interest,
accepts no bribe against the innocent.
Whoever acts like this
shall never be shaken.

Psalm 15 (NABRE)
(JoAnna's sorority's choice scripturE)

As My Best Friend, She Shared with Me

"He answereth and saith unto them, He that hath two coats, let
him impart to him that hath none;
and he that hath meat, let him do likewise."
Luke 3:11 (KJV)

Erica (Best Friend)

I met JoAnna at Wagner College when she came to Rush Week.
But because she had attended college elsewhere for two years,
our college didn't allow transfers to pledge the first semester. With
both of us being from Long Island, JoAnna and I just seemed to
connect; we became instant friends. I wasn't the typical sorority
girl, but I decided to stay in touch with her to ensure she pledged,
and during the spring semester, she did pledge. Later she ran for
president of the sorority.

Joanna was friendly and extremely outgoing, which drew me
out of my shell. She was a fun-loving, beautiful girl with long black
hair, with whom it was easy to hang out and have a good time.
She had an obsession with Betty Boop, and she loved her family
very much. JoAnna looked angelic, sang in church, and was quite
normal. I knew her faults, which were not many. She was my best
friend, and I loved her.

We'd both came to Wagner because we wanted to teach. I'd
always wanted to be a teacher. I came home the second day of
nursery school and told my mother, "I want to be a teacher like
Miss Roberts."

Soon after graduating from college in 1998, JoAnna was
working as a substitute teacher in another school district. After a

year, she was hired as a music teacher in the Comsewogue School District. I didn't have a full-time job yet, so I assisted her by settingl up her classroom and chaperoning her concerts. Her classroom was filled with Betty Boop items. Kids love to know your likes, so they can shower you with theme-related gifts at appropriate times, and they definitely showered Ms. DeSilva with Betty Boop items.

JoAnna made it a personal goal to get me a permanent teaching position. Whenever the faculty would say, "We need a band teacher," she would say, "I know an elementary teacher . . . ."

I'd submitted my resume to several places and received calls to come in for interviews. One day in the summer, because of a late retirement, I was called in for an interview with the assistant superintendent of JoAnna's district and a school principal.

"Did you have any trouble finding the place?" they asked at the end of the interview.

"No. My best friend is JoAnna DeSilva," I proudly announced. "I've helped her set up her classroom and have chaperoned her concerts."

"That's wonderful! We love JoAnna!" (Somehow, I knew they would.)

So, that's how we ended up teaching in the same school district but not at the same school.

Both of our birthdays are in June, so naturally, we celebrated these special days together. We used to say, "You can do no wrong on your birthday. It's your day, so what do you want to do?" Sometimes, I'd just say, "Happy Birthday!" And then I'd ask, "What time am I coming over for cake?" Because my birthday is at the end of June, I normally had a barbeque and would invite JoAnna and her family to come.

Joanna loved hair and makeup, but this was not my thing. We were opposites. She was the one who made kissy faces in the mirror. Once when I was invited to attend a wedding by a guy who would later become my husband, she insisted on accompanying me to purchase a dress. Then, of course, she helped me to get ready by doing my make-up and hair. She did a wonderful job because I married John three years later.

JoAnna liked anything to do with the theater. What drama was referred to in our other elementary schools was a small thing compared to how JoAnna ran her drama club from a performing aspect. Wagner College had had a great theater program, so I'm sure she got lots of ideas from there. I remember JoAnna loved to perform. When you're passionate about something, it's like a magnet, drawing people in. As the drama club advisor, she used a stipend to go all out and create an awesome theater program. She held fundraisers for purchasing costumes and sets. She had real microphones taped to the children's cheeks. The performances she produced and directed with the student actors were large and elaborate for an elementary school.

JoAnna liked all types of music. She sang soprano and enjoyed singing show tunes and church music. Her voice was beautiful and angelic. She also liked regular music, such as pop or rock-n-roll. We used to go out to dance and party. Once I remember we had gone to a party in Connecticut and drove back early the next morning, so she could direct the children's choir at 9:30 a.m. I didn't attend church each week, but I did whenever I spent the night at her house. She was the cantor at Mass and sang for weddings. I remember how blown away I was the first time I heard her sing a solo.

JoAnna and I had some friends who played in a band. We often went to the same bar to hear them. That's where she met Billy, a blonde Harley-Davidson motorcycle-riding dude, who was the bad-boy type that JoAnna was drawn to. She enjoyed riding his Harley with him. JoAnna and I were both good in school and made good grades, but we both dated the boys who were more hyperactive.

I had attended all of JoAnna's students' choral concerts up until 2001. At the time of her winter concert, I was working on my master's degree, teaching, and planning blood drives for my school. I telephoned my JoAnna and explained I couldn't make that night's concert because I was just too tired and overwhelmed with work. She understood, but I soon discovered it was the night Billy proposed to her during the concert. I was so mad at him because he didn't tell me when he answered the phone. I would never have missed that moment.

Once JoAnna and Billy had decided on a wedding date in 2003, and she had asked me to be in her wedding, we both joined Weight Watchers. I ended up losing seventy pounds; JoAnna lost around twenty pounds. We supported each other by making turkey burgers on the George Foreman grill and other diet dishes. She'd have her dad make us breakfast with turkey bacon when I would sleep over, or once in a while, we'd eat his fantastic red meat sauce that is legendary. The sauce cost us many Weight Watchers' points, but it was worth it!

My mom and I were invited to spend lots of holidays at JoAnna's parents' home, which we enjoyed doing. Some of the holidays we shared with them were New Years, Easter, and Christmas. I spent my first New Years with my soon-to-be husband at JoAnna's house, but I didn't spend the last New Years with them. I had bronchitis and wanted to stay closer to home.

JoAnna was the one who brought her family together. She was more of what you'd call a goody-two-shoes. Her brother and older sister were eleven and seven years older than she, respectively; her baby sister, to whom she was the closest, was five years younger. They are a pretty tight-knit family. At the time, the family members lived in close proximity, too. Her brother, Robert, and sister, Angela, still lived in the same town.

Her younger sister became engaged after JoAnna, but she wanted to get married before JoAnna. This didn't upset her sister at all. They had totally different weddings. Annmarie and Jimmy were married at a church with a small reception at the DeSilva's home. JoAnna and Bill wanted the fairytale church wedding, with a catered affair, and a big poufy dress.

I can't remember if I was appointed or if I appointed myself, but somehow, I became in charge of the bachelorette's party. I arranged for a male stripper to come to the house, which was lots of fun. Afterwards, we went to eat at a Hawaiian restaurant because JoAnna and Billy were spending most of their honeymoon in Hawaii.

After JoAnna was dressed in her wedding gown and before we left for the church, the bride announced, while looking in my direction, "I've got to pee."

Of all the times in the world to have to go to the bathroom, I was thinking. But somehow, I got down on my knees and crawled under her dress. There was lots of panicked giggling and laughter. I was the one doing all the work, but I loved her, and she loved me. After all, isn't this what friends are for? Finally, I managed to pull down her blue thong (Something old, something new, something borrowed, and something blue). Now I knew firsthand what was blue. Reversing the process of redressing her was an interesting struggle, as well. So, they were married August 2, 2003, with her sisters as her matrons of honor and me as a member of the wedding party. It brings joy to me to talk about her.

JoAnna and Billy continued living in her parents' home, which had an apartment in the basement. The newly-weds began saving money to build a house. John really liked JoAnna and thought she was nice, sweet, funny, and a good friend to me. But our husbands are both hyperactive types and didn't enjoy just hanging out, so we grew apart after her wedding. We no longer hung out every weekend or talked on the phone every day as we'd done in the past.

On the Friday night when the accident happened, my husband was at a friend's house. At 1:00 a.m. early Saturday morning, I experienced a weird sensation, so I telephoned him.

"I just wanted to make sure you were okay," I said. He told me he'd be home a little later, so I slept soundly.

At eight or nine o'clock Saturday morning, one of JoAnna's friends called me.

"Erica, JoAnna is gone. She died in a car accident."

"No! It can't be true. Are you sure?" I asked. I was in shock.

"Yes. My brother is an EMT (emergency medical technician). He was called to the scene."

"But are you really sure she's gone." I asked, hoping I'd heard this incorrectly.

"Yes. She was DOA (dead on arrival)."

"We need to call Billy's family," I said. I began sobbing. *JoAnna's gone, and I have to call Billy's family.* That's all I could think of. I started taking the phone book out to look for Billy's parents' phone number. John called my Mom, and she came right over to be with me.

We learned the accident had happened two blocks from the house they shared with JoAnna's parents, which was situated on a dead-end street. Ambulances and helicopters were called to the scene, but her parents never heard any of the commotion when it happened. JoAnna and Billy had been babysitting Angela's daughter that Friday night and were returning home.

JoAnna and I both owned Mitsubishi Gallants. That is what she and Billy were driving that night, when suddenly, they were t-boned on the passenger side where JoAnna was sitting. The guy who hit them had stolen the truck he was driving at a high speed. He ran a stop sign and was high on drugs.

I don't remember if I ever got in touch with Billy's parents, but I knew I needed to call the school. So, I telephoned her principal. "JoAnna is gone," I announced.

The school's principal already knew. "Just take care of yourself," she said. I found out later that they conducted emergency faculty meetings to break the news to the staff and to begin preparing for the kids returning to school. They were going to be traumatized when they heard the news.

My mom and I went to the DeSilva home on Saturday and

again on Sunday. My mother had always been a good support-type person. We both wanted to be there for the family. When I saw JoAnna at the wake, she was wearing a white sweater, but it didn't look like her. Her face was different.

I overhead someone telling one of JoAnna's nieces or nephews, "She's just sleeping."

The funeral was crazy crowded.

When JoAnna passed on January 31, 2004, I was devastated. And when it was her birthday again on June 6, I was sad. That's the day John proposed marriage to me. So now, what would have always been a sad day for me would become a happy day. I'd be able to think of it as JoAnna's birthday and the day I got engaged.

Two weeks later I had a mylar balloon from my surprise 30th birthday party. It was half-filled with helium and near my couch. The balloon began drifting slowly toward me until it made its way to my face. I felt this strange vibration, and I saw JoAnna sitting at my dining room table where we always ate and celebrated our birthdays. I like to believe this was a sign from JoAnna on our first birthday apart letting me know she was still with me.

The school held a fundraiser the next winter to raise money for a scholarship in JoAnna's honor. The teachers and faculty had planned a talent show for the fundraiser, but we'd gotten an unexpected crystallized snow that afternoon. When the lights hit the snow, it was like looking at diamonds. It was perfect for my sparkly friend who had been a beautiful girly girl.

"Did you see that snow out there?" Someone asked me.

"Yes. Isn't that crazy?" I responded.

I remember a few of the teachers sang a song from *Wicked,* one of JoAnna's favorite musicals, and the band teacher played a song on drums.

After they caught the man who had stolen the vehicle and killed JoAnna, I wrote a letter to the judge. Many others wrote letters, too, as part of an organized campaign to ask for the maximum sentence for the man who killed JoAnna. Every once in a while, I'll see the file of that letter on my computer, but I've never opened the letter since I wrote it and mailed it. Maybe I should open the file and read it now -- sixteen years later.

I believe it was difficult for JoAnna's parents to stay in their home with all of the memories of JoAnna growing up and living there. For a while, they switched houses with their son, Robert. Then, they moved farther away to Florida where JoAnn's sister lives.

My way of grieving is that I don't like to dwell in the heartache. When I talk about JoAnna to others, I want to share the joyful memories. Sometimes, I don't cry, and sometimes I do. It was hard the first couple of years when we returned to school after summer break because JoAnna and I would always meet on the side and catch up. "Did you hear this?" "No, but I heard. . . ." For years, I remembered every January 31st, but now, the date can slide by, and I don't think about it. But June 6th is the one date I can never forget.

I haven't been back to JoAnna's gravesite since the funeral. I'm not one to go and visit graves. Besides, if I want to talk to JoAnna, I can talk to her anywhere.

Summary
- Try not to dwell in the heartache.
- Share the joyful memories you have of someone.
- Be passionate; it's like a magnet drawing people in.
- Opposites attract; accept others for their differences and admire them for their similarities.

"We have different gifts, according to the grace given to each of us. If your gift is prophesying, then prophesy in accordance with your faith; if it is serving, then serve; if it is teaching, then teach."

Romans 12: 6-7 (NIV)

As a Teacher,
She Changed My Life

"I consider that the sufferings of this present time are as nothing compared with the glory to be revealed for us."
Romans 8:18 (NABRE)

Emily (Former Student / Now Teacher)

Ms. DeSilva sadly passed away on my birthday when I was in the fifth grade. I usually think about her especially during that time of the year. She passed away before she could take the fifth grade to see *Wicked* in New York City as she had planned.

Last year, my mother and I were perusing the Internet to plan what we were going to do for my birthday. We decided to go to Broadway and see *Wicked*. This made me think a lot about Ms. DeSilva. Because it has been sixteen years since her passing, I wanted to see a picture of her. I tried to find a photo myself but couldn't, so I located her sister, Angela. I'd seen an article with her name in it, so I contacted her on *Facebook* and explained why I'd like to see a picture of JoAnna. Angela was touched that I still thought of JoAnna and sent several pictures to me right away. But I could never forget Ms. DeSilva.

"It's so funny that you reached out to me," Angela said. "My parents are having a book written about her. And they are looking for people who can speak about the person she was, how they knew her, and how she impacted their lives." It was almost like JoAnna was with me and pointed me in your direction, Sandi.

JoAnna was so beautiful; I could never forget her. She had the most beautiful long dark hair; her skin was pale, complementing her hair. The lipstick she wore was usually dark or fun-colored.

JoAnna had the most beautiful voice whenever she sang.

Neighbors who were older than my brother and me told us about Miss DeSilva before we attended kindergarten orientation. Then during orientation and while riding the bus, we heard several times, "You will love Miss DeSilva. She is so nice." I remember school personnel took us around and showed us her music room.

I remember the first time I ever saw her. It was September 1998, and she was going to be my music teacher. She was everyone's music teacher from kindergarten until fifth grade. The music room was decorated to look just like her: Betty Boop. There was Betty Boop everywhere. On her piano was a Betty Boop wobble head. There were posters on her walls of Betty Boop and a visible tatoo of Betty Boop on her leg. Her room showcased who she was and the things she was interested in doing. Her beauty stood out.

She was popular with all the other teachers and workers in the building. Anytime you'd see her, she'd be with another teacher, and they'd be smiling, laughing, and talking. I always looked up to her; she was a teacher, who was young and more relatable to us. She was whom I wanted to be when I grew up. I wanted to look like her, sing like her, just be like her. She always wore a smile on her face and greeted each of us by name. She knew every child in the building and got to know us on a personal level as well. You'd find lots of students hanging around her each day. Whenever I think of her, I see her sitting at her piano with a smile on her face and playing a good morning song as she calls our names.

"Hi Emily," she'd say. "How are you? How was your weekend?" Her questions were personal – a way to get to know you. Even when she took attendance, it was like she was getting to know you on a personal level.

I don't remember her ever getting upset or anything like that. If she needed to get everyone's attention, she made her voice louder and would say, "Guys, everyone needs to be quiet." I don't remember anyone acting out or making her mad. Everyone respected her.

Sometime between the first grade and the fourth grade, we participated in *Popcorn Parade* and dressed like chefs and popcorn. I don't know who wrote the skit, but I still remember the silly songs. Parents came during the day to see the skit as we put it on for the other classes. It was fun. My twin brother also was her student. Sixteen years later, he and I still sing the *Popcorn Parade* songs to our family.

If you were in the chorus club or drama club, JoAnna was the director of those, too. By being every student's music teacher, this allowed her to get to know each one on a personal level and determine a way to touch each individual and help him/her find a love for music. Being selected for the chorus club offered special opportunities. We were like a little team of people who shared the same passion for singing. Those students in the drama club had a passion for being on stage and acting or singing for an audience. Those in the drama club were more like a family, more intimate and collaborative. Miss DeSilva's expectations were higher because students had to try-out or compete for a certain role. If you were awarded a lead role in a play, she gave it to you for a reason. She never got angry, but she wanted her students to approach the task with a spirit of "we have to get this done." You knew she was serious about it, while we were excited about it.

Whenever I was awarded a lead role, I wanted to give her my best and make her proud of me. I don't think she had any favorites; she never showed favoritism. But she did enjoy those who were very passionate about singing and acting because they shared her passion. I was one of those people. Naturally, this group was around her more often, doing extracurricular things, and we had the opportunity to grow closer to her.

One year when we performed a winter concert, her husband actually proposed to her. He was dressed like Frosty the Snowman. No one knew who he was or what he was doing on stage. He interrupted the whole concert, took off the snowman's head, and got down on one knee to propose to her. She was surprised and kept laughing because she was confused as to who would interrupt a kid singing a song. She probably wondered if another teacher was pranking her. There were lots of emotions showing on her face before she began crying from sheer happiness. The choral singers and the audience began clapping and cheering. We were so excited for her. It was really cool and became the talk of the school.

We gave another choral program after her fiancé had proposed to her. We sang a medley of older songs to celebrate her engagement. She was on Cloud Nine. One of the songs we sang was, "Going to the Chapel." I'm so glad we did.

We performed one play per year. We gave it during the day for the other classes in the school and again at night for all the parents. The year I was in the fourth grade, we performed *Music Man Junior.* I didn't have a big part in the play, and that bummed me out, but she talked to me and told me, "Don't worry. This doesn't mean you aren't good. Just maybe you need to work a little harder."

So, I worked super hard the next year, and I got a lead part in the play *Grace, Mr. Warbucks's Secretary.* It was a big deal for me. She gave me that part and gave me lots of accolades. I was proud to have pleased her.

"See? Remember last year when you were so upset you didn't get a big part?" she asked me. "You've improved so much. You've earned it."

I was happy because she had acknowledged my improvement and hard work. I was growing in my passion and doing a good job. So, when we performed *Annie* that year, she gave a couple of other people and me a strand of costume pearls for us to wear as we had the bigger parts in the play. I kept mine and didn't return them. I felt so cool that I had a piece of her that she personally gave me to wear in the play. I have them to this day. I don't know if anyone ever asked for them back. I just took it she had given them to me. That makes them special. I feel the pearls were a true representation of JoAnna; the color of her skin was delicate, prominent, and beautiful.

I remember the last day I saw her. It was the day before my birthday. In elementary school, if a student wanted to celebrate his / her birthday, he / she were allowed to bring treats, such as cupcakes for the entire class. My mother brought my brother and me cupcakes from a bakery to distribute to our class. If we had any left over, our teacher allowed us to go to anyone in the school we wanted to and give him/her a cupcake. Once I saw that every student had received a cupcake, I asked permission to go and give cupcakes to other teachers. Of course, I headed to JoAnna's room first. I was so excited to give her one of my birthday cupcakes. When she saw me, she stopped her class, walked to the piano, and played "Happy Birthday." She and her class sang to me. That made me so happy.

I asked her, "Do you want a cupcake? I have an extra one for you."

She said, "No. But I'll give you a hug." That's the last time I saw her.

Someone called the next day to inform our family she had passed away. I vaguely remember snow being on the ground that Saturday morning. My brother and I were outside playing when our father called us in.

My dad sat us down to tell us. We were so devastated. I think everyone had a unique relationship with her. I felt closer to her because I was in drama club, so I had stayed after school with her. I was also in the chorus, so I worked hard because I was very passionate about singing and had sung solos during music concerts, so I felt very connected to her. My brother was very upset. He had a unique relationship with her, too. He was passionate about chorus and drama, like me. She gave him the Laundry Guy role who carried Annie in the laundry basket. He was also the understudy for Daddy Warbucks and was super-stoked about that. If the person playing that part had been sick, my brother would have been able to play the part, but the person never got sick.

Miss DeSilva had been my teacher for six years. With her being so young, it was a shock to realize she had passed away. I'd never thought someone so young could die, especially since I had just seen her yesterday and everything seemed fine. She had sung me "Happy Birthday," and had given me a hug. I couldn't fathom such a vibrant person, one so full of life dying so young.

We begged our parents to take us to the wake. "Please! We want to say goodbye." It was a big deal for us to have closure. But I had never been to a wake or a funeral before. Mom knew my personality; she knew it would scare me.

Mom discussed it with Dad several times and kept telling us, "No, it's not a good idea. You don't want to remember her this way." But they finally realized how important it was to us, so she and Dad relented and drove us to the funeral home.

There was an overwhelming number of people -- students, family, friends, people I knew, people I didn't know, and her husband was in a wheel chair. I told him how sorry I was, but he seemed out of it. It was apparent from the huge crowd how many lives she had touched. Everyone must have felt a compelling need to be there for her and her family.

When I saw her in the casket, it was the first time I'd ever seen a dead person. I didn't know what to expect. In a way it looked like her; in another way, it didn't. She'd been killed in a car accident, so the funeral home people had tried to make her look as she did when she passed. I was shaken. Mom had been correct. She knew I shouldn't have gone. But I thought of it a lot afterwards and realized I needed the closure and opportunity to say goodbye. Now, I'm really glad I went because it meant a lot to her family and me that her students would come and pay their respects.

I was angry at the man who had taken her life. I was angered that someone could not have a care in the world for other people and only think of themselves. The man had taken this bright light from the world. Now she was gone because of his bad decisions. After I'd seen her at the wake, I mentally shut down and didn't want to know any more about the apprehension and conviction whenever it happened. I didn't want to know any more about the legal end.

Afterward, we had a male music teacher, which was definitely different. I was unfairly disappointed because he wasn't Miss DeSilva. I felt that he wanted to move on without giving us time to grieve. He thought he was distracting us by doing different things. He didn't want us to dwell on the sad things. I wish he had allowed us to talk about her after she passed away. Other counselors spoke to us and other teachers allowed us to talk about her and grieve her death. Some allowed us to write about her. Her former classroom was filled with even more Betty Boop items and flowers. It became her shrine.

We did perform *Annie* that year. Another teacher had taken over the drama club. Some of the teachers helped us prepare for the play. We worked hard and were proud of the end result even though Miss DeSilva wasn't there, but her husband and family came to see the production. We felt as if she were there, too, because she should have been there. The best thing we did was to perform the play in her memory.

If I could summarize her life, I'd say she really loved children and music. She wanted to pass on that love and passion for music to others. I really believe she inspired me to become a teacher. Her love for what she did -- teaching and knowing children on a personal level impacted me as a person. She made other people feel special and important. That's how I want to be remembered as a teacher.

I value my students as individuals. I believe love and passion come from your heart. It's the type of person you are. Some teachers aren't patient or as caring. To be an effective teacher, you have to love it and want to do it, or it is obvious to your students and others. Your job has to be your passion. I've had plenty of teachers who were more interested in retiring or just having a paycheck.

I never told JoAnna I wanted to become a teacher even though she was a big part of my decision to become an educator. Her warmth as a person was constant with her genuine greetings for each of us and her desire to know us personally. I learned from her; I was inspired by her. Even though I'm a special education teacher and not a music teacher, her kindness and passion for children is something I want to model and pass along to other people, too. That's why I chose teaching as my career.

Summary

- Use your gifts according to the grace that has been given to you. If it is teaching, then teach.
- Show each person that he / she matters; be interested in others and get to know people personally.
- Call people by their names; people want to be recognized and acknowledged by others – especially those whom they respect and care for.
- Don't be afraid to smile. A smile is always better than a frown.

"Charm is deceptive and beauty fleeting;
the woman who fears the LORD is to be praised.
Acclaim her for the work of her hands, and let her
deeds praise her at the city gates."

Proverbs 31: 30-31 (NABRE)

As a Fellow Educator, She Taught Me About Friendship

"Pleasant speech multiplies friends,
and gracious lips, friendly greetings."
Ben Sira 6:5 (NABRE)

Bonnie (Teacher and Friend)

I worked with JoAnna at Boyle Road Elementary School. We both began teaching there the same year, so we became friends right away. I noticed she had a Betty Boop tattoo on her leg, which made me think, *What a fun and happy person. She's so positive!* In addition to us, two more educators began that year, as well. Fortunately, Sharon and Nicole had similar personalities, so the four of us clicked, being the *newbies on the block.*

JoAnna was a down-to-earth person who was easy to talk to and someone who was always interested in your day or whatever was going on in your life. We all felt comfortable opening up to each other. Sharon and Nicole were closer to JoAnna's age, and I was older, but it didn't seem to matter.

I taught special education during the time I knew JoAnna. When I think of her, I see an open, happy, smiley person, who made me feel wonderful whenever I dropped off my special education students in her classroom for their music lesson because I knew she loved and cared for them like I did. She'd greet me and each student with her beautiful smile.

There were times when you had a special area teacher who does not understand special ed kids. It made me sad to drop off my students to those teachers. With JoAnna, it was the opposite.

I felt as though I were giving my students to someone who understood them. If there was a problem, she was willing to look at the positive side of it. For example, if a kid was misbehaving or acting out, she didn't see it as a negative. Rather, she'd say, "This is what we had happen today. Let's see what we can do to make it better."

The four of us (JoAnna, Sharon, Nicole, and I) had lunch at the same time each day in the faculty room. It was a time to catch up on life and see how each person's day was going. On Fridays, if possible, we'd go out to a nearby restaurant for lunch to celebrate the end of the week.

I remember when Billy proposed to her during the winter concert. It was the talk of the school. She was so happy. I felt fortunate we had the opportunity to experience that special moment in her life!

When JoAnna began planning for her wedding ceremony and reception, we were swept up into her excitement and happiness, eager to hear about all the stuff she was going through. I never had thought JoAnna needed to lose weight, but she'd joined Weight Watchers. I believe she wanted to look her best in her wedding dress. It was fun hearing about all of her wedding plans.

Nicole, Sharon, and I went together to JoAnna's wedding. When I saw her coming down the aisle, I thought, *How beautiful! Her face is radiant. She looks like she is glowing.* She was the embodiment of happiness; her smile was radiant and never left her face from the beginning throughout the night. It was easy to see how happy she was. Reminiscing now, I'm grateful she experienced this moment in her life. God was good to allow her that.

It was obvious to anyone who knew JoAnna that she was very close to her family. I don't remember meeting her family prior to the wedding. By me being older and with kids, I was unable to participate in a lot of outside outings with Sharon, Nicole, and JoAnna. I do remember how happy all of her family was on her wedding day! Her wedding was amazing. She couldn't have been more beautiful and joyful. Of course, being with her on that special day was icing on the cake for me.

Our principal, Maureen, called me when she died. I was devastated because I couldn't believe someone so full of life could be taken so early. She had begun talking about having babies and all the things to come. I felt very sad she was cheated out of it, and I'd lost my friend.

Someone would need to clean out her classroom, but no one wanted to do it because everyone was so devastated. Finally, the principal asked me if I would clean out JoAnna's desk and her classroom. She wanted me to pack up her personal things, so her family could have them. I was devastated, too, but I allowed myself to become as numb as possible. I remember initially crying, crying, crying as I removed things from her desk drawers. I knew the items would be important to her family. In the midst of the dreaded task, I chose a different spin by realizing how privileged I was to be chosen to touch her things, which helped me to smile through the tears quite a few times. True, it was sad she wasn't with us anymore, but her items shouted her gleeful personality and that she had been here. It was a special place where she had worked and taught and cared and loved.

After a while, it became a happier task. I was honored to do this for JoAnna and her family. I removed things from the bulletin boards and the tops of tables and the piano. I was proud the principal had asked me to perform this task, even if it were quite soon after hearing the tragic news. Some of my friends were too overwhelmed to even go inside the classroom, which I could totally understand. But it was obvious the school would need to get substitute teachers scheduled.

When I finished packing everything, I thought of JoAnna. This had been emotional, but it had been quite touching, too. It made me feel as if I still had a connection with her after she was gone. I felt as though JoAnna was saying, "It's okay. I know you're sad, but it's okay." I didn't know her family well, so I handed the boxes to the principal. Either she or Erica would return them to her family. They both were closer to JoAnna's family.

I went to the wake and saw more devastation on everyone's faces. Her friends and family members were a mess. Children were bringing flowers and other things to place in the casket with her. It was totally a senseless way for her to go. It happened out of nowhere – horrendous.

All of us were walking around in shock. Children were in shock; it was hard for us to explain why she wasn't there. They had given us the words to say and assistance ensuring we were saying the correct things. There were psychologists available to help. We had to deal with ourselves being upset first, so we could be there for the kids.

We were given the opportunity to have a substitute, so we could take the day off if we wanted to attend the funeral. Several of us did, and afterwards, we assembled at a diner where we sat and talked about JoAnna and how amazing she was. We expressed our sadness and shared advice about how to get through this sad time. It was a catharsis to go to the diner and grieve together. We knew we had to deal with our own emotions before we could help others.

I was thrilled when the responsible person was captured. Perhaps there would be justice now. As a collective group, we wrote a letter to the judge, pleading for the maximum sentence possible. This man had senselessly taken our JoAnna -- a joyful person who was full of life and enjoyed doing fun things. I can't think of one negative thing about her and have never heard anyone else say anything negative.

Before the accident, whenever she wasn't at lunch with us on Fridays or in the faculty room, we missed her greatly. Out of concern, it never took us long to discover why she wasn't there. JoAnna was the life of the party and lit up any room she entered. Just seeing her smiling face made you happy, too. Her constant desire to find the positives in life was contagious.

I'm a religious person – a Christian -- who believes in angels. Without a doubt, JoAnna was an angel from the first moment we met. She is still an angel. I think of angels as being happy people who bring positives into other people's lives. Sometimes I wonder if she died because God needed her in Heaven.

JoAnna's shoes couldn't be replaced as a music teacher. We had so many substitute music teachers after she passed away. In addition, she'd directed the plays and concerts – anything musical. I remember the way she looked at the kids in chorus. She'd smile and they'd respond to her positive energy. She was a special person and friend.

Nicole (Librarian and Friend)

JoAnna was a very positive happy genuine and real person. She was down to earth – a straight shooter. JoAnna and I were very close colleagues and friends at Boyle Road Elementary School. We were hired the same school year. People who are hired together seem to form a special bond that lasts forever. Once we became friends, we figured out our dads knew of each other from work, too.

We were having a pajama day at school. Can you believe Joanna and I showed up wearing the same style of pajamas? They were blue and white cloud pajamas. So, one of us wore the top and the other one wore the bottoms. Everyone assumed we had shared the pair of pajamas because we were close friends, but we actually had no idea what the other one was wearing until we showed up to school that morning. Great minds think alike.

I'll never forget sitting in my jeep that day during our lunch period together (unfortunately, also a few hours before her accident) and her telling me that she and Billy were going to start a family. I'll never forget that early morning phone call from Arlene, the art teacher and JoAnna's mentor, telling me about JoAnna's accident and passing. I'll never forget the sound of her mother gasping in the funeral parlor as I entered her wake that night. I'll never forget one of our students, walking up to her casket and saying, "Yep. They got it right except for her nails. She would never wear that color. Her nails always looked nicer than that." I'll never forget walking into that first faculty meeting after JoAnna's accident and that feeling of emptiness.

On Monday morning, the weekend after JoAnna's passing, one of our colleagues walked into her classroom to find a beautiful swallowtail butterfly flying around the room even though it was February. She ran to get me and show me the butterfly. She had heard of butterflies being a symbol of the Resurrection. When we went to JoAnna's wake, we saw that beautiful silk butterflies had been placed all over several of the arrangements. We saw it as a sign that our friend was okay.

Every time I see anything Betty Boop or anything with a butterfly, I think of my friend.

Sharon (Teacher and Friend)

JoAnna, Bonnie, Nicole, and I started at Boyle Road Elementary School the same year. We were the new kids on the block, who bonded right away. We just clung to each other being the newbies. JoAnna stood out from the *get go*. She had beautiful long black hair, deep ruby red lipstick, and red nails. She was very bubbly and outgoing with a zest for life. She seemed to embrace every minute of every day and make the most of life. When I first met her, one of the things she spoke about was her love of Broadway plays. From that time forward, whenever she went to a play or I went to a play, we'd find time to discuss it. She recommended I go to see *Wicked*, and I did. I've actually seen it five times because it is my all-time favorite show.

I started out teaching kindergarten, but when I was pregnant with my daughter, I taught first grade half a year. Then I was back to teaching kindergarten, which I have taught for twenty-one years. Kindergarten kids are amazing. It is the best grade in the world to teach. They come in and are so excited about learning everything. My morning starts with hugs and receiving pictures they've drawn for me. From September to June, I have the privilege of seeing their growth. Once a week, I took my classes for music. The kids loved going to music classes and hearing JoAnna sing. They loved the songs that she taught them and would return from music happily singing the songs she had taught them. JoAnna had a beautiful voice and had put together a CD, including two songs that she sung on. One was just of her singing, and one was a duet with her brother-in-law.

JoAnna loved all things Betty Boop. She had Betty Boop designs in her classroom. Whenever I see Betty Boop, I take that as a sign from her. For the first few years, Nicole, Bonnie, and I would find Betty Boops and send them to each other or purchase three of them and place them in each other's school mailboxes. On the anniversary of her birth or death, we used to send each other pictures of Betty Boop or emoji hugs – Thinking of You.

JoAnna was already dating Billy when she came to work at the school. Shortly afterwards, they got engaged, and she was planning her wedding. She was so excited to go on this journey. She loved her church and was very involved in her church. JoAnna was never embarrassed by her dedication to it, which some people unfortunately are. She talked proudly about who she was as a person and never hid any part of herself. When I saw her on her wedding day, she was lit from within -- so happy.

On the Friday before she passed in the wee hours of Saturday morning, she told me she and Billy were going to look at houses that weekend. As soon as they purchased a home, they were going to start trying for a family. We were excited together. My daughter, Gillian, was already born. JoAnna had visited her when she was a baby. She realized how exciting this part of life was and couldn't wait to get started on her own journey of having children.

While growing up, I went to St. Jude Church until I was thirteen. JoAnna and I didn't know each other at that time. When we arrived at the church for her wedding, I said, "St. Jude is where I was baptized and made my first Communion and Confirmation." It was strange being in that church again, and even stranger being in that church five months later for her funeral. It's one of the most heart-breaking things I've had to deal with in my lifetime.

On the day of her death, my husband, Austin, daughter, Gillian, and I had dentist appointments. Our dentist's office is located by his mother's home in Levittown, so we stayed there that day, returning home around 7:00 p.m. There were several messages on the answering machine from Maureen, our principal at the time. There were also calls from the school psychologist. In the messages, Maureen had asked, "Can you give us a call when you get in. Some things are going on we need to talk about."

Right away I knew something bad had happened, so I called Maureen's home, and her husband answered. "She's not home right now."

"Roy, something has happened. Can you please just tell me?"

He said, "I know she wants to talk to you."

"Roy, I just need to know. I know something bad has happened."

He paused before saying, "JoAnna was killed in a car accident."

I remember standing in my bedroom and then falling to my knees and crying. My husband and Gillian were walking down the hallway. When Gillian saw me on the floor and crying, she said, "Mommy has a boo boo." She'd assumed I'd gotten hurt.

My husband asked, "What happened?"

I told him, "JoAnna was killed in a car accident."

Austin said, "Oh my God! Oh my God!"

A few months earlier, a group of us had gone to a comedy club. The group was JoAnna and Billy, Bonnie and her husband, my husband, Austin, and me, Nancy and her husband, and Caroline and her fiancé at the time. Austin, of course, knew JoAnna from

101

attending her wedding.

There is a special song from *Wicked,* "Because I Knew You (I've Been Changed for Good)." The day after JoAnna passed, I was listening to that soundtrack when that song came on. When I heard it, I just broke down and cried because it reminded me of her. To this day, I still think of her anytime I hear it. The teachers and faculty all met at the school building the next day to grieve together. Everyone was crying and sharing special anecdotes about her.

I visited Billy in the hospital the same day. He was a broken man. As soon as he saw me, he kept repeating, "I couldn't save her; I couldn't save her. I didn't see him at the corner."

I hugged Billy and assured him, "It's not your fault."

"It was my fault. I was driving," he cried.

"But you couldn't stop."

I'd heard the criminal was driving at a high rate of speed in a van he had stolen. He was drunk and did nothing to try and stop. After the crash, he ran from the scene.

"I was screaming for help," Billy cried, "and I could hear him running away."

After that day, when the teachers and faculty met at the school building to discuss JoAnna and to grieve together, it seemed like a black cloud hovered over our school building for years. It was like a cancer, the beginning of sadness. There were many untimely deaths and terminal illness diagnoses in the years after JoAnna's death.

I attended JoAnna's funeral. Afterwards, several of us met at a nearby diner to tell stories about JoAnna and to laugh. We needed this time to regroup together.

We joked about the substitute music teachers. After JoAnna's death, we'd have a string of horrible music teachers. It was as if JoAnna was saying, "Nobody's going to take my place." It actually took ten years for them to find another music teacher that was "good enough." However, no one could ever quite fill her place or produce the beautiful concerts she did. Yes, JoAnna was saying, "Nope, you are not filling my spot."

On January 19, 2005, we held a concert to raise money for a scholarship in JoAnna's name. A bunch of us from Boyle Road Elementary School sang, "I'd Like to Teach the World to Sing," in her memory. We had printed the words on the back of our program with a large picture of Betty Boop in case we forgot the words. Two music teachers, who knew her well, sang the song from *Wicked*. A high school music teacher gave a drumming performance using garbage cans with some of her students.

JoAnna was funny and beautiful like sunshine. She loved to sing. No one in our school building could ever say a bad thing about JoAnna at any point. She never made anyone angry, and I never saw her angry. No matter what was going on, she was always positive, never down. She never had a mean thing to say about anyone. She could always see the light in any situation. Things that might frustrate or annoy other people just didn't bother JoAnna. She made you feel better just being around her.

If JoAnna were here with this Coronavirus, she would say, "Don't worry. We're going to be okay. Enjoy the time with each other and your families." She'd be at home singing.

It has been wonderful talking about JoAnna for this book. It has brought up a lot of happy memories I haven't thought of in a long time.

Summary
- Enjoy time with each other and your families.
- Make others feel special by showing interest in their lives and passions.
- Don't be angered.
- Turn negatives into positives.
- Always see the light in any situation.

"Your work is going to fill a large part of your life, and the only way to be truly satisfied is to do what you believe is great work. And the only way to do great work is to love what you do. If you haven't found it yet, keep looking. Don't settle. As with all matters of the heart, you'll know when you find it"

Steve Jobs

As an Employee and Teacher, She Was Joyful

"I keep my eyes always on the LORD. With him at my right hand, I will not be shaken. Therefore my heart is glad and my tongue rejoices; my body also will rest secure."
Psalm 16: 8-9 (NIV)

Maureen (Principal)

I worked with JoAnna for quite a few years, and she was amazing. There is something unique about music teachers because they organize performances for the children's families to enjoy. It's common for music teachers' own families to attend, as well. When you're a principal and work with teachers, oftentimes, you don't know anything about their families or have a chance to meet them. But when you work with music teachers, it seems you always get to know who their families are. For JoAnna's students' concerts, her parents were always there. I met her parents many times and some siblings, and I got to meet Billy. JoAnna was more than just a teacher I saw at work because I got to see the depth of her family's love.

JoAnna was passionate, enjoyed working with children, and loved music. She wanted students to have that joy in their lives. She was really effective at reaching the children and connecting with them. The children worked hard to be good at whatever they were learning, in particular, the musicals. JoAnna and her students presented such a high quality of entertainment. The musicals were beyond the level of an elementary school because of her passion and how the children responded to her as a human being and teacher.

Everybody loved JoAnna. She was funny, vibrant, and energetic. Her energy was sparkling. She always wore a smile on her face and was fun to talk with. She possessed a unique role in the elementary school. Each teacher normally has twenty to twenty-eight children in the classroom. JoAnna was the only classroom/vocal/music teacher; she taught every class and connected with around five hundred students. It was extraordinary. She knew each child's name.

There are not many teachers who got to speak to all the teachers in the school each week, but because of JoAnna's unique role of providing classroom music instruction to every class, she did. She performed her role well by being caring, extremely talented, and knowledgeable. And she had a beautiful voice. Whenever she would sing the "Star Spangled Banner," at each of our graduations (promotions) and other special events, people would always comment; it was amazing to hear.

JoAnna became engaged at school; it was exciting for the students. Her boyfriend, Billy, planned it all after receiving permission to propose at the winter concert. He borrowed our Snow Man suit, which one of the teachers wore each year. Billy came out dressed as Mr. Frosty during the audience sing-along. JoAnna was definitely surprised by the Snow Man interrupting the concert and proposing marriage to her. Billy adored her. At her bridal shower, colleagues, friends, and school personnel were all there.

JoAnna had a larger than life personality that can be described as really fun, sparkling, and passionate. The children loved her. In addition to her ability to communicate and build relationships, she was also an excellent musician. The students were taught many things about music. She brought her heart and soul to everything she did. And JoAnna was funny. There were times when she got exercised if something wasn't the way she thought it should be to ensure a successful performance for the children. Her passion led her to express whatever it was, along with solutions; she was *all in* all the time.

In addition to being our classroom music teacher for all the classes, she was the choral teacher for grades four and five. The chorus was optional, but JoAnna always had a big following. She also arranged for students in other grade levels to have special performances. She was an incredible force – so devoted.

JoAnna was full of ideas, always thinking of something amazing for us to try when running special events like Flag Day or thinking about exciting ways to do something. Music enhances every aspect of the school, so anytime there was an event, JoAnna would come through with creative ideas for the children to enjoy.

I had the sad task of breaking the news of her tragic death to others at the school. I telephoned each person individually because I knew it would be so devastating. On the following day, which was a weekend day, we opened the school building and came together in an attempt to help each other. All of us were in shock, but we wanted to begin thinking of how to help the children. The loss of any life is devastating, and for children to lose their teacher is very difficult. In this case, every child was JoAnna's student, and all our Boyle Road students were impacted. We focused on the messages to give children and how we would help them through this. We also discussed behind the scenes, which was how we would help each other. There were some tough things and difficult decisions to make -- emotionally and mentally. For example, do you let classes go back to JoAnna's music classroom? If so, how soon? We did what we thought would be best for the children, each other, and JoAnna's family.

We telephoned her mom, dad, and sister to let them know we were thinking of them. There was a huge outpouring of sympathy; students and staff wanted to express their love for her. We tried to manage each idea and suggestion to honor JoAnna's spirit and joy. I can picture JoAnna smiling with her long hair and love for Betty Boop.

I believe her spirit is very much alive. My favorite moments with JoAnna were working together at graduations (promotions). She and I would meet to plan the ceremony, which always began with entrance music while the children marched in. Next, JoAnna would sing the "Star Spangled Banner." Everything would be quiet and calm while we listened to her extraordinary soprano voice. Afterwards, the fifth graders would perform a song. There were so many times during those events when JoAnna and I would make eye contact while I was on the stage and she was sitting at the piano on the floor to the right of the stage. She was just so magical and brought joy to the kids.

To honor JoAnna's memory, each class created a memory quilt page that assembled into a book. It was absolutely beautiful. We shared it with her family when we dedicated the playground equipment to JoAnna. The staff held a memorial concert in JoAnna's memory with many performers. A group of staff members formed a choir and performed while holding Betty Boop pictures.

I'm grateful I knew JoAnna and that this very special person and her parents have been part of my life. I have occasionally seen JoAnna's parents when out in the area; it's always good to see them. They've had such a difficult road. I'm glad they organized this project. This book will be a beautiful celebration that demonstrates how important each life is. We may never know how many people we influence during our lifetimes.

And aside from being special, I believe JoAnna was in fact an angel.

Summary

- Don't settle on a job or career; look for what you enjoy doing.
- Love and be passionate about whatever you do.
- Caring teachers can make a world of difference in their students' lives.
- Remember how a smile can impact another person.

My Auntie
by George Naylor

When I was hopeless, you were there.
You picked me up; you showed me care.
Without the love you had for me
God only knows where I would be.

To me, you were a second mom,
A person I drew wisdom from.
In my corner every fight,
You always cared that things were right.

I won't forget the things you've done.
I felt like your adopted son.
Ready now and feeling new,
I couldn't leave not thanking you.

As My Aunt,
She Taught Me How to Love

"Why did I not listen to the voice of my teachers,
incline my ear to my instructors!"
Proverbs 5:13 (NABRE)

Brian Anthony Zippel (Nephew)

While I was growing up, Aunt JoAnna was one of my best friends. She was always there for me – like an angel. She was definitely the glue of the family. When she passed away, I was fifteen years old and in the eighth grade. You would think a family would draw closer, but everybody is farther apart.

Aunt JoAnna and Uncle Billy had only been married six months. They were just starting their lives together. She'd become a successful music teacher, and he was my best friend; we did everything together. I was honored to be an usher in their wedding.

My aunt was beautiful with dark hair like most of us in the family. She had brown eyes – a beautiful person all around. When she passed, she was around the age I am today -- thirty. Sadly, she didn't have the opportunity to live as long as I have. My aunt was taken too soon. I don't think it was her time to go, but I guess God has a plan for everybody. I'm sure He had a reason for taking her when He did.

Aunt JoAnna and I used to do fun stuff like going to the movies when I was young. She was outgoing and motivated -- a wonderful person with a positive attitude. My aunt knew what she wanted early in life, so she went to college to prepare for achieving it. JoAnna was someone I could look up to as a young person. If I'd grown up with her in my life and she hadn't passed away, I feel

I'd be a different person in a good way. She definitely had a big impact on me. Having her in my life to confide in would have been a good thing.

On that dreadful morning, she and Uncle Billy had been babysitting Samantha and left our house around 3:00 a.m. They were supposed to stay over that night, but Aunt JoAnna wanted to go home. I knew if I didn't stay awake and ask them to "please stay, don't go," they would leave. But I fell asleep and didn't wake. My next memory is of my mother screaming.

I shared a room with my big brother, Rob. I looked over at him and asked, "Do you think something has happened to Aunt JoAnna and Uncle Billy?"

"I hope not," he said. But we both knew something bad had happened from the way my mother was crying. I asked Rob if I could climb into bed with him. He said, "Sure." They came to wake us at 7:00 that morning, but we hadn't been able to get back to sleep. Our parents told us Aunt JoAnna had been killed in an accident, but Uncle Billy had survived.

People like Aunt JoAnna are hard to find. She was the first person I ever lost. I think I get my goodness from her. I try to be a genuine and loving person. I don't like to see anyone getting hurt or things going wrong. Aunt JoAnna was just a wonderful person, who touched everyone's life. She is my idol; I want to be just like her.

She sang at the church during Mass and sang for other venues. Her voice was wonderful – actually, it was amazing. I can remember riding with her in the car, and she'd turn on the radio. This was in the '90s. Listening to that same music now evokes good memories. Betty Boop was her favorite character, so I kept a sticker of Betty Boop on my wall to remind me of my aunt for a long time.

I tend to be a procrastinator, but if she were alive today, I wouldn't be; she wouldn't have allowed me to be because she believed in getting things done. Aunt JoAnna influenced me in good ways. Her advice was simple: "Follow your dreams."

I absolutely feel her presence at times and am certain she is my guardian angel. And yes, I believe she was an angel on earth who was sent here to show people how to love. That's why we're all here -- to prepare for Heaven. She deserves this book, and I'm excited about it.

Summary
- Remember life is about preparing for Heaven.
- Try not to procrastinate.
- Follow your dreams and prepare yourself for them.
- Show others how to be positive; promote "goodness" and "positivity."

Happy 1ˢᵗ Birthday in Heaven JoJo, a wife, daughter, daughter-in-law, sister, sister-in-law, aunt, niece, cousin, granddaughter, teacher and especially a friend, was taken from us the day your life ended so abruptly. We will never forget your beautiful smile, your beautiful voice. They are cherished in our memories forever. Not a day goes by that you are not thought of. God must have needed a special angel because that is what you are. Forever our angel, we will always love you.

Your Husband Billy,
Mom, Dad and Your Family

June 6, 2004 (Newday)

As My Daughter, She Influenced Many

"Do not fear: I am with you; do not be anxious: I am your God.
I will strengthen you, I will help you,
will uphold you with my victorious right hand."
Isaiah 41:10 (NABRE)

JoAnn DeSilva (Mother)

On Friday nights, JoAnna went to the church to practice for Sunday Mass. So after practicing on January 30, 2004, JoAnna and her husband, Billy, went to babysit little Samantha for Angela. I had telephoned JoAnna at Angela's, but my grandson told me she was sleeping. I was going to tell her to just stay at Angela's house that night and not bother coming home, but I never had the opportunity to speak with her. On their way home, just two blocks away, the fatal car accident happened. I don't know the details of how JoAnna died, but my husband does. I couldn't deal with it other than to know it was a car accident, and the person ran away.

Our son, Bobby, helped his father make the arrangements When she was at the funeral parlor, I couldn't bring myself to go inside and see her, so I stayed in the front area. I was there physically but still in shock and broken-hearted. I remember a touching moment, which I'll never forget. While I was sitting outside the parlor, a little boy stepped up to me and said, "Thank you for giving birth to JoAnna and for putting her in our lives."

I'm told there was a long line of people who waited an hour or more to pay their respects for our daughter. Her funeral Mass was held at St. Jude on February 5, 2004. She was laid to rest at Mount Pleasant Cemetery, Center Moriches, New York. The only

114

time I've been to the cemetery was the day of her funeral, and I've never been back again. I didn't want to see her gravesite, so the funeral directors drove the car in an opposite direction on the street, so I didn't have to see it. They were very kind to me.

Honestly, I don't know how I dealt with it to tell you the truth. If I hadn't believed in God or had my faith, I think I would have rolled up and died with my daughter. I never would have made it. And that's the truth. I thank God for giving me the strength and fortitude to keep on placing one foot in front of the other.

I also believe God placed Annmarie's husband in her life at the right time because when JoAnna passed away, Jimmy was there to comfort and support Annmarie, who still misses and grieves for her older sister. God sent him for her, and I'm thankful. I wasn't able to comfort anyone – not even myself.

I couldn't deal with going to court, so I never went to the courthouse for the trial or sentencing, but my husband, Bob, did. I marvel at how my husband was strong enough to do all that he had to do when I couldn't help him. I never felt hatred for the man who did it, but I didn't want to know who he was or his name. If JoAnna were alive, she wouldn't begrudge or hurt anybody, so I try to follow my daughter's example.

I am thankful for and blessed to have my other three children, grandchildren, and two great-grandchildren even though I think it's a shame God took JoAnna when He did. Why? Because she didn't get to have children. She was so happy to become a wife and wanted to have children. Otherwise, our daughter lived more and accomplished more in her twenty-nine years of life than many people do in a lifetime.

My grandson, Brian, who is Angela's son, was a young teenager when his aunt passed away. He strongly believes her spirit has protected him and saved his life many times when he was doing something wrong. I, too, feel her spirit is with my family. JoAnna's passing was a huge loss for our entire family. Her death changed everyone and the lives we live today. Holidays and celebrations are different because we feel her absence. My children and Bob and I live in different states, so it isn't always easy to get together at special times.

I don't believe JoAnna's husband could cope with her death, and maybe we reminded him too much of her. He just left all of us, which was very sad for me. I've never blamed Billy for her death even though he was driving the car. My daughter would never have wanted me to do that. I believe God wanted her in Heaven, so He took her.

After JoAnna's passing, Bob and I received 169 letters from children and former students she'd taught from kindergarten to the fifth grade. They wrote about how JoAnna had touched their lives and what she meant to them. JoAnna was the type of person who loved unconditionally, like a mother loves her child. It didn't matter what you did or said or if you embarrassed her, it didn't bother her. She was a special person.

In addition to the letters, notes, framed pictures of JoAnna, and drawings, her students made two themed quilts with sixty-nine squares each. They were about JoAnna's life. They gifted Bob and me with one quilt, and they gifted her husband with the other quilt. Boyle Road Elementary School created a plaque that read, "In Memory of JoAnna." Bob and I had the privilege of cutting its ribbon.

JoAnna's friends and co-workers held various fundraisers to create a music scholarship in her name. With other funds, a children's outdoor playground and swing set were dedicated at the school in JoAnna's name. Every year we award a scholarship to someone who excels in music. We are able to do this because of the money people and our family contributes. Over the years, donations have decreased, but we're still able to collect enough donations to keep the scholarship going.

Of course, when she passed, Bob and I went to talk with our priest. He knew JoAnna well; she sang for Sunday Mass and other occasions in the church, and she led the children's choir. He sat us down because my husband and I were crying. He spoke with us, attempting to comfort our pain and fill the huge holes in our hearts. When our priest said, "I have two angels whom I pray to – my mother and JoAnna," that's when I knew how much he loved her. It was beautiful and unbelievable when he shared those words with us.

Whenever someone passes away, a frequent comment people make is, "He/She was special" or "He/She was the best person in the world." All I can say is JoAnna makes those words meaningful, more profound, and poignant because the truth is JoAnna was extraordinarily special to many, many people – not just to Bob and me.

Her precious life has positively impacted my life, my husband's life, and her siblings' lives. And she impacted the lives of friends, students, co-workers, parents, performers, and so many others. I just didn't realize the influence our daughter had on other people. That's why I don't want anyone to forget about JoAnna. Those who didn't know her can be introduced to her now through the pages in this book. My purpose for this book is to remind people there are good people out there, just like JoAnna – not just the bad people. I want my daughter's memory to live forever.

Summary
- Positivity impacts and influences your life as well as other's lives.
- Try to love unconditionally, like a Mother loves a child, like our Father in Heaven loves us.
- Your faith and belief in God will get you through the darkest times. Lean on Him for strength, comfort, and guidance.
- Don't hate; hatred is destructive.

"Peace I leave with you; my peace I give to you.
Not as the world gives do I give it to you.
Do not let your hearts be troubled or afraid."

John 14:27 (NABRE)

As My Sister,
She was an Angel on Earth

"Cast all your worries upon him because he cares for you."
1 Peter 5:7 (NABRE)

Robert (Bob / Bobby) DeSilva (Brother)

When they finally arrested the person who is responsible for killing my sister, I recognized his name once I heard it. This man and I weren't friends or acquaintances, but I knew who he was. He and I are the same age. The District Attorney had told our family the man responsible for the car accident was going to jail for twelve years because he had other offenses.

As I sat there looking at the back of the criminal's head, my mind kept echoing the same words over and over again. *He was driving high and stole the truck that killed my sister. No one was chasing him. And after he slammed into their car, he left the stolen truck sitting there and ran away. He killed my sister. What a coward!*

While Dad, Angela, her husband, Bob, and I attended the trial, we discovered this guy had been in and out of jail, like it was a revolving door. I couldn't fathom living with myself after an accident took someone's life, but apparently, he could. He was the type who never learned a lesson. He just kept on doing whatever he wanted.

Fortunately, someone had ratted him out a month later after the accident. The rumor was that his mother wanted to kill that person who told on him. If true, this was just another example of our society and people being raised not to accept responsibilities or to be accountable for their actions. Raw anger surged throughout my

119

body as I sat there in the same room with this criminal. If I didn't believe in Jesus Christ and feel His hands on my shoulders holding me back, I couldn't have stayed in that courtroom and listened to the defense's excuses, hear about his extensive criminal record, and see the pictures of the accident scene without ....

Students, parents, teachers, community members, family, and friends had written countless letters to the judge, asking for the stiffest sentence possible. Apparently, he had taken their words to heart. On the day of sentencing, the judge actually cried and said, "I wish I could give you more time than what the law allows for what you took away from this earth." He was sentenced to fifteen years in prison. But can you believe it? He won an appeal and served only eight years. My parents didn't learn about this until later. Even after he was sentenced and served time for my sister's death, he committed another stupid crime and was sent back to jail. What an idiot!

After the sentencing was over, it took me a while, at least a year, to recover my faith, which I'd always had. I can't comprehend why that temporary loss occurred. Maybe it's because I was grieving or couldn't understand why JoAnna had to die. Maybe it was my pent-up anger. There was plenty of it, so maybe it replaced my faith in Jesus Christ. Maybe I was just exhausted physically, mentally, and emotionally. All I know is I felt lost and empty, only I wasn't lost. God still watched over me.

Now more than ever, I believe there is a battle between good and evil that is constantly going on all around us. In the spiritual sense, it's more than a battle; it's a war. We have to become stronger believers and withstand the slew of temptations and easy sins that test our faith constantly, as the untimely and tragic loss of my sister tested mine.

Over the years since she passed, something miraculous or inexplicable happens to increase my faith in Christ. I've also come to believe that there is a time for all of us to move on to Heaven or to be returned to earth. I believe God, Himself, is the One to tell you, "Stay. You're not going back," or "Go back. It's not your time yet." God needed JoAnna, so He told her to "Stay."

We are reminded of her often. There isn't a day when my family and I don't speak of her. My mother meets people in Florida who knew JoAnna. It's a small world, but JoAnna made it even smaller by reaching out to all four corners of the earth, country, city, and community and by meeting and caring about so many people.

Several years after her passing, I was standing in our backyard, just looking up at the clouds. Sometimes, I'm sure you've seen different shapes that reminded you of something or somebody. But this time, I could see Jesus' face clearly, along with a verse, Luke 24:10. I had forgotten all that had happened in the church during JoAnna's funeral when I'd opened the Bible to read the name *Joanna.* I hadn't written down the passage as a reminder. What does this mean? So, I Googled Luke 24:10 again, and it was the same verse I had read at her funeral when I needed comfort. I took it as a reminder that Jesus and JoAnna's spirit were always with me.

These days, I try to be happy and not angry. I strive to be more like Jesus, the way JoAnna did. She was an angel and the closest thing to being a perfect human that I can think of. And I'm not just saying this. I always felt there was something special about my sister. There was a glow around her.

I miss my parents, who have lived in Florida for a year. I long to travel to see them whenever I get enough money. My two children, Bobby and Brianna, are grown. Brianna just had my grandson, Giovanni. Bobby is a teacher now, like his Aunt JoJo. He also coaches football, which I did when he was coming up. They were nine and ten years old when their Aunt JoJo died. And Rosalie's two boys, John and Antonio, are grown, too. They both knew and loved their Aunt JoJo.

Unfortunately, I lost contact with Billy, not on my part. Somehow, it just happened. Maybe he was advised by a grief counselor to get away from our family because of the painful memories. After the accident happened, Rosalie and I took care of him. He'd sustained broken ribs and a punctured lung. They'd airlifted him to Stoneybrook the night it happened. I love the guy and would love to see him again.

I am limited because there are no known words to express how great a person she was. The feeling is indescribable. JoAnna was alive the year I turned forty. She gave me a surprise birthday party at my parents' home. The whole family was there, including my wife Rosalie, who was my girlfriend at the time. JoAnna met Rosalie and loved her. She used to tell me, "You better marry that girl." I did – in 2005, unfortunately, after JoAnna was gone.

I've learned to slow down, look around, and appreciate a lot more in my life. I want to be more like Jesus, the way JoAnna was. We were a lot alike in the good parts. JoAnna would have gone on to greater things, even greater than what she'd already done. She was kind, giving, and caring -- always wanting the people around her to be happy. I miss her a lot, but she'll never completely go away. She'll always be alive in my heart and memories. My sister was just an angel – truly.

Summary
- Try to be happy and never angry.
- Strive to be more like Jesus.
- Slow down and appreciate the moments and people in your life.
- Try to make other people happy.
- Be kind, giving, and caring of other people.

Letters from Students and Others

"When you call me, and come and pray to me,
I will listen to you."
Jeremiah 29:12 (NIV)

Our Hero
You are our hero.
Thank you for your gifts.
Your smile.
Your love.
Your talents.
We will miss you.
We will make you proud.
Your memory will fill us forever.
Love,
Your past and present students

Over 169 students' letters and cards, along with letters from parents, faculty, school administration, and friends, were received by JoAnna's parents and her husband in the days and months that followed JoAnna's untimely death. Their numerous and heartfelt words expressed many of the same sentiments as listed below and on the next page.

- JoAnna was a special person who is greatly loved and is missed.
- JoAnna lived a wonderful life and influenced them to

follow their dreams.
- Their thoughts and prayers were with the entire family.
- They shared in the family's loss and grief.
- There were no words to express their sadness and pain.
- JoAnna touched the lives of everyone who knew her.
- JoAnna always wore a beautiful smile and had a great attitude that lit up the room with her presence.
- "God put her down on this earth to enrich the lives of everyone she knew."
- JoAnna had a wonderful family.
- JoAnna had a positive influence on their lives.
- JoAnna is one of God's angels.
- They were grateful to be in her life and to know her.
- If not for JoAnna, "I wouldn't be a physician's assistant today."
- If not for JoAnna, "I wouldn't be a teacher today."
- JoAnna was an awesome drama teacher, chorus teacher, and music teacher.
- JoAnna will be remembered forever.
- JoAnna will never be replaced.
- JoAnna was a talented, beautiful lady who sang like an angel.
- JoAnna is a spirit and an angel and taught us how to play the recorder and to enjoy the *Popcorn Parade.*
- If it weren't for her help, "I wouldn't be acting today."
- "Your daughter motivated me and inspired me to sing. I do believe your daughter is an angel."
- "She should have gone to *American Idol* because of her voice."
- JoAnna was a role model.
- "If you believe in Heaven and God and angels, she is an angel up in Heaven with God and all the other angels."

The following letter was written by a student named Brittany, who graduated in 2001. It is a perfect summary for this section.

Dear DeSilvas and Billy,

Mrs. DeSilva touched all of our hearts so much! She was always smiling. I remember going to her class and just enjoying her company and music. I am so sorry for this horrible tragedy. She didn't deserve to die. But for some reason, God needed another angel with a great heart like Mrs. DeSilva.

I try to think of all the good times. I remember in drama club my cell phone rang because my dad needed to know where I was, and I thought she was going to get mad, but she just laughed and said, "I didn't get my cell phone until like fifteen." I also remembered how devoted she was to us and the drama club. She made our costumes, which were so cute! I thought it was so nice of her to take the time to make our outfits.

She loved Betty Boop. I think her room was filled with Betty Boop. I wish I could have seen her more! I remember the last time I saw her. It was for my brother's graduation last year. She was the only teacher that remembered me. She also was the only teacher I cared about. It made me feel so good that she remembered me. I know that she was loved by everyone who walked into her room. She uplifted my spirit and made me want to go to school. Mrs. DeSilva always made funny faces at us on the risers, so we would laugh.

It's not right at all for what was done, and I am so sorry. I do know everyone is saying they are sorry to you guys, but I want you to know that this is coming from my heart. Mrs. DeSilva was one of the greatest people I knew. She motivated me to fulfill my goals. I had her the first year she was there [Boyle Road Elementary]. Whenever I saw her in the halls, she always said, "Hi."

I remember when I was in, I think, fourth or fifth grade, and I was in drama. My brother was in the second or third grade, and he had to stay with me during drama. So, Mrs. DeSilva let my brother sit at her desk and play with his Gameboy. She was the most caring, loving, and happy person I've ever met. She wasn't just my teacher. She was my friend. She cared about us and never lost hope in us. She has touched my heart and left me with a great sense of life.

Mrs. DeSilva was a great person, and I loved her so much. I remember when Billy played Frosty and would kiss her good luck before each concert. I am so sorry for you guys. She was a wonderful person. . . .

Letters to the Judge Prior to Sentencing

"I have told you this so that you might have peace in me. In the world you will have trouble, but take courage, I have conquered the world."
John 16:33 (NABRE)

Parents, students, co-workers, church members, priests, school administration, friends, and family wrote letters to the judge, pleading for the stiffest sentence possible for the man who killed JoAnna. Some of the letters are presented here. As you read the selected letters, notice how each one paints a lovely description of this cherished woman.

Dear Your Honor,

Before you sentence the man who took the life of JoAnna Berggren, please consider the great loss the Parish community has felt since her death. JoAnna was an inspiration to the people of this community, especially to the children. Thank you.

To Whom It May Concern:

On the morning of January 31, 2004, our lives were changed forever by Chester Cunningham. He caused a very bad accident and also left the scene of the accident. When it was all over, our niece, JoAnna Berggren, had lost her life and our nephew, William Berggren, was seriously hurt. JoAnna was a very warm, loving young lady who we loved very much. Our nephew, William Berggren, her husband, lost his wife of only five months at the age of twenty-nine years old. JoAnna was our son John's best friend. He was their best man at their wedding. JoAnna had so much in life to offer everyone who came in contact with her. She was a school teacher. Music was her life. She had a beautiful voice when she sang. She directed the children's choir in church. She also sang in church on Sunday mornings. All the children loved her. Our family has been torn apart tragically since all this happened.

Chester Cunningham has a very bad criminal record for all that he did and caused. He's only receiving 6 ½ years to 12 ½ years. Where is the fairness in our justice system? Chester Cunningham is getting a slap on the wrist. He deserves life with no parole. Our hearts are broken and nothing will bring our niece JoAnna back and mend our nephew William's broken heart.

To Whom It May Concern:

Joanna and our son William were only married five months. They were just starting their life as husband and wife. They were in the process of buying a house and starting a family.

JoAnna was an elementary school teacher who taught music. She also was a cantor at St. Jude Roman Catholic Church.

On the night of January 31, 2004, returning home from babysitting their niece and nephews, they were hit by a hit and run driver. Joanna was killed and William was hospitalized with five broken ribs.

At JoAnna's funeral, the outpouring of support from students and parents that came to show their respects for her was astounding. The amount of people this woman touched in a short life shows the kind of woman that was taken from us.

My wife and I will deeply miss Joanna. I will not use the word accident because this definitely was a deliberate disregard for human life. Mr. Cunningham deserves the maximum sentence allowed in this case, which will never be enough.

To Whom It May Concern,

My brother, William Berggren, asked me to write a letter to

you about his wife JoAnna. This is a difficult thing for me because I have been thinking for days what to write. I guess I should just tell you about JoAnna.

JoAnna was a very beautiful young lady whose life was cut way too short too soon. Joanna was an elementary school teacher. Joanna taught her students music. Her students loved her. At her funeral, the children lined up to see her and say goodbye with tear-stained faces and sad looks wondering why they were saying goodbye to her. She was a cantor at St. Jude Roman Catholic Church where she sang on Sundays. She also taught the children at church to sing beautiful songs at church.

JoAnna put everyone else first. The night she was killed, she was babysitting her niece and nephews. William and Joanna were married August 2, 2003. They were just settling into being a married couple. They were looking for a house to buy and talking about starting a family. JoAnna wanted to have a baby so bad, but they were waiting to have a family. My brother would have been a great father. I watched my brother on their wedding day. He cried as soon as she walked down the aisle. He cried through their vows. It was the happiest day of his life. He was going to spend the rest of his life with JoAnna. That was supposed to be a good fifty years or so.

Everyone suffers from this. JoAnna's mom and dad, Mr. and Mrs. DeSilva, have put their house up for sale and have moved to Florida because of their pain. They cannot bear to live in their home anymore. Every corner of that house is filled with JoAnna.

Everyone wonders why this happened. Why was JoAnna taken from us? She was such a wonderful person, so filled with life and love. Her family and my brother are all trying to pick up the pieces and move on as best as they can. The pain that fills my brother's eyes and heart is unexplainable. My brother is in therapy trying to deal with his pain and grief.

The cause of everyone's pain is Mr. Cunningham. Mr. Cunningham is the man who stole a vehicle and hit my brother and wife's car on January 31, 2004. He was in a residential neighborhood. His deliberate actions caused everyone's pain. This man left my sister-in-law and brother to die and did not look back. He did not turn himself into the authorities. He is a criminal. He does not have any consideration for human life and no consideration should be shown to him. I hope you sentence him to the maximum, which will never be enough of a punishment for this man.

To the Honorable Judge Hudson,

Five months after I sat in St. Jude Church celebrating the wedding of my friend and colleague, JoAnna Berggren, I sat in the same church for her funeral -- Five Months Later.

JoAnna's life was full of joy and giving. We started teaching the same year, and she was one of the finest teachers with whom I had the privilege of knowing and working. The children loved her. I cannot emphasize this enough. The children adored and loved her. They simply loved going to her class to hear her sing. JoAnna touched their hearts and their minds with her music, her warmth and her smile.

Her devotion to music and others didn't stop at teaching in school. She was also the director of the choir at her church. She sang at Mass every Sunday.

My last memory of JoAnna is a conversation we had at school the day before she was killed. She was telling me just how happy she was. She was married to a wonderful man. She had a richly rewarding career teaching music to children. She was telling me how she and Billy were getting ready to look for their own house and that she couldn't wait to get pregnant and have a child. JoAnna told me that she felt like all of her dreams were coming true. She felt like her life was just beginning.

When you sentence Chester Cunningham, I ask that you take what I have written into consideration. I understand that nothing is going to bring JoAnna back to her friends and family and all of the children whose lives she has touched. We all miss her terribly each and every day. But by giving Chester Cunningham the maximum sentence allowable by law, you will ensure that he never takes away someone as special as JoAnna Berggren again. Please don't give him the opportunity to kill again.

Your honor, thank you so much for taking the time to read this letter.

Dear Judge Hudson,

Chester Cunningham took away my Aunt JoAnna DeSilva Berggren. He stole a vehicle from Holbrook and drove to Shirley. Chester drove through a stop sign and ran into my aunt. After that morning, all of my family's hearts have been cracked in half. If you ask me what you will call this person, I would call him a coward on the bottom of my shoe. Some people might think who cares if someone dies but my Aunt JoAnna was not a someone. She was an angel on earth, but now, she is an angel in Heaven. So, if you really think about it, our whole family has a big chunk of their hearts lost. He should never come out of jail, or he might destroy another family.

Your Honor:

To lose a child is the worst thing a mother and father can possibly go through. To lose a child because of the actions of an irresponsible selfish imbecile makes it that much worse. As I sat in the courtroom when this pathetic dope plea bargained, I could not help but wonder why he was being asked how fast he was going, although he could not be asked if he was drunk, coked up or both, while driving a stolen vehicle through stop signs. Certainly, he was going fast enough to end a wonderful giving and caring person's life. Although we realize that the penalty could not be longer, no penalty could ever suffice for the taking of our daughter's life. We want to see this moron behind bars forever! But this is not going to happen; we will have to settle for as long as the law will allow. I am not going to enumerate all my daughter's many accomplishments or sit and think about all that she meant to so many people and how this void can never be filled. It is just too painful to contemplate. She truly was an angel on earth and God's gift to everyone. I know it sounds like a cliché, but in this instance, it could not be truer.

Mr. and Mrs. Robert DeSilva

Your Honor,

As Halloween approaches, I think about what my sister JoAnna would have worn this year. You see, every holiday was special to JoAnna, including Halloween; this picture was taken last year, the last one I would take of my sister and daughter, Samantha, (her godchild) together dressed up on Halloween. JoAnna dressed up every year to make Halloween special for the children she taught at school and for her nieces and nephews. They all loved seeing her dressed up. This was the type of person she was. I thought we would have many more years to see all of her wonderful costumes, but no this is the last one she wore. Why? Because Chester Cunningham stole a truck for his drug endeavors, sped through a stop sign in a residential area, and left my precious sister and her husband to fend for themselves. He just left them there. There was no remorse. He is not sorry for what he has caused. This amazing person is not here any longer because of his irresponsible choices. He should not have any more choices. He should be paying for this with more than what he is going to receive. I know the laws should be changed, and I wish every day that someone will change them so another family does not have to go through the pain and anguish JoAnna's family and friends and students are going through. This man has been in trouble with the law since he was a juvenile. Why does he still get a chance when my loving sister JoAnna and her husband Billy have none?

Please your Honor, I ask you to give this man the longest

possible sentence you can.
Angela Zippel (Sister)

To Whom It May Concern,

My name is Breanna DeSilva. Last year Chester Cunningham stole my Aunt JoAnna's life. Since she passed away, everybody has been crushed. Even children in school also have been crying and falling apart. She had touched so many lives, and I don't understand how he can take her life away and just run away.

She was a music teacher and was a chorus teacher and also sang in church every Sunday. Some people don't understand how many people she touched and how much she will be missed. People at the school she worked at are doing so much for her.

Chester Cunningham took away my Aunt JoAnna and a big chunk out of my whole family's heart. So please leave him in prison for as long as you can. Don't let him hurt someone else's family! Breanna DeSilva (Age 10)

To Whom It May Concern:

My sister, JoAnna, was my best friend since the day I was born until she was ripped away from me on January 31, 2004. I am supposed to write what impact her tragic death has had on my life. Well, I don't know where to begin. My life can never be the same; she wasn't just the greatest sister any one could ever ask for, she was the greatest person I ever met. She always took care of me and everyone else. She always did the right thing her entire life. She was so compassionate and loving to everyone who came across her; I always said she was an angel on earth. She never did anything wrong; she always followed the rules. She lived an amazing life, a life every human should strive for. She was full of goodness and love. Her family meant so much to her. She always went out of her way to make sure we were all taken care of. She was everything that the Bible tells us we should be. She touched so many people's lives at such a young age. People don't live a whole lifetime and achieve what my sister did in her short one. It is so unfair that her wonderful life was cut short by a monster who has no clue what he took away from the whole world. This world was so much better with my sister in it. There aren't too many people like her. In fact, I can't name one. People just felt good to be in her presence.

I will never again know true happiness. I miss her so much. I cannot believe that I'll never talk to her again. She was my sister and my best friend. My whole life I always tried to be more like her, but I could never do it; she was so special. She never got angry or upset with anyone; she only saw the good in people. Ever since she was born she was always smiling. She was the happiest person; she loved life. She worked very hard to get all the things that she wanted out of life, making others smile along the way. She, of all people, deserved everything she wanted out of life, but it was torn away from her.

It took months for me to go back to a "normal" life, just to go back to work. I cry every single day. The one thing I used to love to do was listen to my sister sing, and I can't even bear it now. I don't think I'll ever be able to again and it kills me. I still cannot believe that I will never hear her beautiful voice again or see her smile. I wear a picture of her smiling on a necklace around my neck just to remind me of how happy she was. I don't know if I'll be able to live the rest of my life without her. We never even got into a fight. All of my memories are with her, and they are all wonderful.

I can't even bear to look at pictures of my family before this tragedy. To see my parents smiling and my nephews and nieces, I miss that. This has torn my family apart. JoAnna was the rock in our family. We all meant so much to her. I don't even know how we'll get through the holidays; they were so important to her. She loved giving, and she loved her family.

It will never get easier; it's only been getting harder. My parents can't even live in their home anymore, being how close the tragedy was to the house. Everything has changed and it's horrible. I miss her and until the day I die, I will. My life is so empty without her in it. I still can't believe that she's gone. I really don't know how we are going to go on.

I would like to apologize if this letter is jumbled, but this is very hard to put on paper.

Annmarie Marchisotto (Sister)

Your Honor,

I am truly grateful for the opportunity to write you this piece on behalf of the late JoAnna Berggren and her family.

In February of this year, the irresponsible action of Mr. Cunningham suddenly took away from us one of the most beautiful leaders we have in our church and thus, dealt a chilling blow to our faith community here in Saint Jude, where our grief is still very fresh because JoAnna touched all of us in a way that cannot be easily forgotten.

It just got to our attention that the gentleman who perpetrated this heinous crime is up for sentencing and that the possibility exists for him to be paroled halfway through his sentence. That was very painful for us to hear because, your Honor, we believe that this gentleman is a danger not only to himself, but also to the rest of us and to innocent law-abiding citizens everywhere who might just chance to be close to him.

It is with this grave concern that we implore you to hand Mr. Cunningham the full sentence that he and the rest of society deserve.

We thank you for all your work in providing peace and justice to innocent people everywhere, and we pray God to continue blessing you.

Rev. Joseph Baidoo

To Whom It May Concern,

So, a life has been taken. Life will go on for him, won't it? He will serve his sentence, come out of jail, go home to visit his family and friends and simply pick up where he left off. This is the kind of criminal that apparently will never learn his lesson. He has been in and out of jail for years. His time spent in jail in the past does not prove worthwhile to this individual. When someone goes to jail, it is my understanding that they will spend time reflecting on the crimes he/she has committed and to rehabilitate. This has NEVER worked for him. He left prison in the past simply to choose to continue to commit crimes. Now, he has taken away the life of an incredible woman and the heart of an amazing family. But yet his life will go on.

JoAnna Berggren, on the other hand, will never again be seen by her family or friends – what did she do wrong? Nothing – and her sentence is death. Did she know she was going to die? Her life had just begun. She'd been married for just a few months and was looking forward to becoming a mother. As a teacher, she touched the hearts of hundreds of children that have felt this loss deeply. She babysat her niece and nephews who lived just blocks away – and two blocks from her house, she was killed. I wonder if she saw the light lit on her mother's front porch as they were driving up the block. I wonder what she was thinking or saying at that very moment when her car was hit. Funny thing is we will never know. We will never see her smile or hear her voice at the church choir again. I look at pictures of her, and she looks like an angel. Did this really happen?

While a pained family searched for answers and feared that this man will strike again, he remained at large for months without a care in the world. He simply went on; he never even stopped to see if his victims were ok, without any regard to human life. Why should he be spared? Why should he be given the chance to do this to another family?

There are people who go to prison and come out changed every day; former gang members preach to local youths about the dangers of this lifestyle; ex-drug/alcohol abusers come out and devote their time to others to try and prevent others from leading their kind of life. This individual, after coming out of prison on numerous occasions, only chose to continue his way of life. He has been in and out of correctional facilities, and as his record shows, he cannot be corrected. And now look what he's done. The problem is not with the way the system works; the problem is with this individual who will never learn his lesson. He should not be spared. He needs to be kept away from innocent law-abiding civilians. Everyday he is not behind bars is a day that another family will be at risk. He didn't even stop to care about the regards of people whose life he took with his bare hands. Why would he ever care? Why would he care about anything? It could have been his own mother or sister in that car that night. He would never have known; he just went on. I don't know who will read this. I don't know if anyone will ever even see this, but whoever reads this, consider this. If this was your daughter, what sentence would you feel this individual deserved? Take a moment to think about this. This could have been your sister or mother – consider that. Consider that no sentence would ever justify what he has done. Have no mercy on this individual; he had no mercy on JoAnna, a human being. Why should anyone have mercy for him? He has been given way too many chances already, and this is what has happened. He took the life of a little innocent girl, an angel – a family, along with a community, is devastated and this person goes on living without a care, without any regard, and that's it. I can't ever imagine there being a day that I will go out somewhere and actually have the possibility of bumping into this person. I can't even imagine what that could feel like. Seeing him breathe, walk, talk, perhaps even smile, when JoAnna Berggren, my friend, will never walk the face of this earth again. I just don't understand how this person could actually be let out of jail one day.

This will be a year of many firsts: her first birthday, Thanksgiving, Christmas, her one-year anniversary that never came. It should also be the first year this person is in jail for the rest of his life because JoAnna no longer has life.

News Articles

In an article, "HIT & RUN: THE DRIVERS, THEIR VICTIMS AND ONE LOOPHOLE IN THE LAW" written and originally published by Billy Jensen in January 2005's edition of *The Numerous Solutions of Billy Jensen* and posted again on August 20, 2013, in *Archives*, he exposes a loophole in New York's law regarding hit-and-run tragedies (www.billyjensen.com) that would have impacted the laws and sentencing when JoAnna's accident occurred.

HIT, RUN AND HIDE

Whether they're aware of the law or not, hit-and-run drivers who are intoxicated are actually rewarded by the law for running away instead of staying at the scene. Drunk drivers who flee the scene of an accident face smaller penalty s (A Class E felony, up to four years in prison) than if the driver stays and waits for the police to arrive, takes a Breathalyzer test and is proven to be intoxicated (a Class D felony, up to seven years in prison). Earlier this year, elementary school music teacher JoAnna Berggren, 29, was riding with her husband William in their 2001 Mitsubishi Galant on a road in Shirley when a white Jeep Cherokee ran a stop sign and struck the car, killing Berggren. The driver of the Jeep then pulled the car over and fled on foot. The Jeep had been stolen from a Verizon company repair yard in Holbrook earlier that week, the Verizon logo painted over. The driver was identified as Chester Cunningham, 39, who had a history of DWI convictions. If Cunningham was drunk this time, he will escape homicide charges because he fled.

It is a loophole that many lawmakers and advocates have been aware of for years, but has yet to be closed.

In the same article, Jensen quotes Deena Cohen, then president of the Long Island Chapter of Mothers Against Drunk Driving, who addressed the New York State Assembly in 2012.

"'Most hit-and-runs are drunk drivers," says Deena Cohen, president of the Long Island Chapter of Mothers Against Drunk Driving. "We're basically giving them permission to leave the scene and sober up.'"

After Jensen published the story again in 2013, a law was passed, which made fleeing the scene of an accident resulting in serious injury or death a Class D felony.

"A Lesson in Mourning for Children"
Nedra Rhone
February 3, 2004

In the sunlit lobby of Boyle Road Elementary School, parents lined up, as they do every morning, to see their children off to class. They exchanged hugs, kisses and quick waves goodbye before teachers led students, single file, to their classrooms.

But yesterday, along with their stuffed animals, lunch boxes and rolling backpacks, most children at the Port Jefferson Station school also carried the knowledge their music teacher, JoAnna Berggren, was gone.

Berggren, 29, died in a car accident early Saturday, just blocks from her Shirley home. A driver in a stolen Jeep ran a stop sign and hit the car in which Berggren was riding with her husband, William, police said. William Berggren, also 29, who was driving at the time of the accident, remains in the hospital with broken ribs and a punctured lung. Police are still looking for the suspect or suspects, who fled on foot.

Officials in the Comsewogue school district learned of Berggren's death later Saturday morning. The news reached most of the school community through a telephone tree initiated by District Superintendent Richard Brande. "We got the call on Saturday morning," said Leandra Mas, wife of school board member Eric Mas. "It was really quite shocking." Mas's children, ages 8 and 11, asked if they would see Berggren again, Mas said. It was their first experience with death.

"I encouraged them . . . to feel free to talk to the teachers, to give other kids a hug and to realize that everyone is feeling the same way," Mas said.

Some students expressed their feelings in handwritten letters and posters they brought to school to decorate the door of Berggren's classroom. Berggren had been at the school for about six years and most students had been in her class, in the choir, or in the drama club, Mas said. This year, Berggren's students were planning to perform the musical *Annie*.

"Crisis management teams met during the weekend to determine how to assist staff and students," said Shelley Saffer, deputy superintendent. "Counselors were at the school yesterday," Saffer said, "and would be available at least until the end of the week."

As they arrived yesterday to meet with Principal Maureen, teachers greeted one another silently, offering hugs and tears in place of words. To students, they offered smiles and tender hellos. "Our children look to us for answers," said Vicki Maskulyak, a parent volunteer who helped students exit cars and buses yesterday morning. "How do we explain it when we don't understand it ourselves? I just tell them, 'She is an angel.'"

"Mastic man accused in teacher's death"
Jennifer Sinco Kelleher
March 15, 2004

140

Six weeks after a mysterious hit-and-run driver left a newlywed schoolteacher dead and her husband injured in Shirley, Suffolk, police Saturday arrested a Mastic man who they said crashed into the couple with a stolen Jeep.

The early morning January 31 crash killed JoAnna Berggren, who taught music at Boyle Road Elementary School in Port Jefferson Station, and seriously injured her husband of five months, William Berggren.

Police arrested Chester Cunningham, 39, in front of his home at 2 Wills Avenue Saturday afternoon. Det. Sgt. Timothy Dillon of the Seventh Squad said he could not reveal details of what led police to Cunningham. The investigation is continuing and detectives are asking anyone with information to call Crime Stoppers at 800-22-TIPS.

The Berggrens, both 29, were just three blocks from the home where they lived with JoAnna's parents when the driver of a stolen Jeep Cherokee ignored a stop sign at the intersection of Tyne and Lexington Roads, slamming into the passenger side of their 2001 Mitsubishi Galant. The driver of the Jeep abandoned the vehicle and ran, police said.

JoAnna, who was in the passenger seat, was pronounced dead at Brookhaven Memorial Hospital Medical Center. Her husband, who had broken ribs and a punctured lung, was released about a week later from Stony Brook Medical Center.

JoAnna Berggren's brother, Robert F. DeSilva of Mastic, said yesterday the family is relieved. "He couldn't be man enough to stand up to what he did," DeSilva said. "To say, 'Hey listen, I made a mistake.' He didn't do that. He had to be caught. To talk about him makes me sick," DeSilva said.

Cunningham was charged with leaving the scene of a fatal motor vehicle accident and third-degree criminal possession of stolen property "because the Jeep was reported stolen from a Verizon facility in Holbrook," Dillon said. At his arraignment yesterday, Cunningham pleaded not guilty to those charges in

First District Court in Central Islip. He was ordered held at Suffolk County Jail in Riverhead in lieu of $25,000 bail. His next court date is Thursday. Cunningham's relatives could not be reached for comment yesterday.

Dillon said Cunningham is a landscaper with several prior driving while intoxicated and larceny arrests. Police did not have the disposition of those arrests available yesterday. Records show he served prison time for grand larceny but it was not clear for how long and when.

Dillon declined to say whether police had any indication that alcohol was involved in the crash. JoAnna's husband was too distraught to speak about Cunningham's arrest, DeSilva said.

DeSilva said he wants his sister remembered as a gifted singer who was devoted to teaching children. She was choir director at St. Jude's Roman Catholic Church in Mastic Beach, where she sang at Mass every Sunday. At her school, she was also drama director. "She put on plays at Boyle Elementary that high schools couldn't do," DeSilva said. "My sister was a lot more than just a school teacher," he said. "She was a mentor to hundreds of kids. She did nothing but good for everyone."

"COPS BUST L.I. MAN IN FATAL HIT-RUN"
At 5:00 a.m. on March 15, 2004, Selim Algar posted his article online.

A Long Island man has been nabbed in the horrific hit-and-run that killed a young newlywed and seriously hurt her hubby in January, cops said. Chester Cunningham, 39, of Mastic had eluded Suffolk Police for six weeks before being busted Saturday near his home, authorities said.

Police said Cunningham was the driver of a stolen vehicle that slammed into a car operated by William Berggren, 29, at an intersection in Shirley on Jan. 31.

The crash killed Berggren's new wife, beloved elementary-school teacher JoAnna Berggren, 29, who was a passenger in the car.

Cunningham was charged with leaving the scene of a fatal accident and criminal possession of stolen property (www.breakingnews.com).

"They Found the Driver who Killed JoAnna Berggren!"
At 8:14 a.m., March 15, 2004, *LI Weddings* (*Long Island Weddings*) posted the following article written by IrishTracy.

Police say they have arrested the driver who struck the car of a popular Shirley music teacher and left her to die. JoAnna Berggren was killed in January.

Cops busted hit-and-run suspect Chester Cunningham of Mastic, charging him with leaving the scene of a fatal motor vehicle accident. Detectives say the 39-year-old landscaper was driving a stolen Verizon Jeep when he plowed through a stop sign at Lexington and Tyne Roads in Shirley and slammed into Berggren's car. The impact killed 29-year-old JoAnna and seriously injured William Berggren, her husband of five months. Cops say Cunningham then fled on foot.

Berggren's brother says the family is too distraught to speak on camera about the arrest, but he issued a statement saying nothing is going to bring his sister back, and the family wants Cunningham prosecuted to the fullest extent of the law.

Cunningham is also charged with possession of stolen property. Police say he also has a record of several DWI and larceny-related arrests as well as other convictions.

"Vermont's DNA index gets first 'hit'"
John Zicconi, Vermont Press Bureau, Waterbury
April 28, 2004

When David and Ann Scoville's daughter Patty was brutally

raped and murdered in Stowe nearly 13 years ago, the New York couple turned their sorrow into action. Because Patty's killer was never found but left biological clues behind, they campaigned relentlessly for Vermont to establish a DNA data bank that would be linked to the FBI's national DNA Index System.

The Scovilles still believe that DNA profiling will eventually lead to the arrest of their daughter's killer. The local DNA bank was established in 1998 with much fanfare, but it took until this month for Vermont to celebrate its first match. A "hit" was finally recorded April 16. The data bank linked biological evidence found this February in Dover to a fatal hit and run traffic accident that happened a month earlier on Long Island.

The accused criminal, Chester Cunningham, 39, of Mastic, N.Y., was arrested in March and is now in a New York prison awaiting trial for manslaughter, assault and leaving the scene of an accident. He pleaded not guilty, but is being held in lieu of $750,000 bail.

He faces up to 15 years in prison for allegedly running a stop sign and killing a 29-year-old elementary school teacher. Although this crime does not involve Patty Scoville's killer, her parents were overjoyed Wednesday to learn that Vermont's DNA data bank is finally bearing fruit. "We worked an awfully long time to hear that," David Scoville said when he heard about the success. "It's just one hit, but it can multiply from there. It will give them reason to keep going and expand the bank. "The more samples we have, the more chance we have of solving crimes," Scoville added. "This is one of the things that does work. We were so active in getting the bank established for the very simple reason that we believe is the way we are going to solve Patty's murder." Vermont law enforcement officials were equally excited. "This is a case-to-case hit that linked two different crimes together," said Eric Buel, director of the Vermont Forensic Laboratory.

"This is very cool. It's a first time for us." Despite its six-year history, Vermont's DNA data base is still a work in progress. Local officials have processed biological samples from nearly 1,200 convicted felons, but have done little with so-called "no-suspect" samples even though about 300 have been collected statewide. No-suspect samples are obtained from crime scenes where the perpetrator is unknown.

DNA is collected from blood samples, cigarette butts and a host of other objects and then placed into the data bank with the hope that someday it will match either evidence from another crime scene or a sample obtained from a convicted felon. Federal law requires that those convicted of violent crimes, such as rape, murder, assault and burglary, provide DNA samples for the data base.

Nationally, 1.7 million samples are in the FBI system. Crime labs from 50 states and 32 countries participate in the program, which has generated more than 13,000 hits and aided nearly 17,000 criminal investigations. An average of 10 new hits are generated each week, FBI officials said. Vermont State Police officials said Cunningham's blood was found along with skis, televisions and snowboards that were stolen from the Mt. Snow Resort in Dover. Police say Cunningham also stole a car from Deacon's Den, a Dover bar, and fled to New York. Vermont's crime lab has entered just 20 of its more than 300 no-suspect DNA samples into its data bank. However, the Waterbury lab recently received a $250,000 federal grant to send an additional 45 samples to an outside facility for processing. The money also allowed the lab to purchase a robotic DNA extractor and hire two employees to process additional samples in house. The Vermont lab has a backlog of about 1,500 samples taken from convicted felons.

Senior forensic chemist Peg Schwartz said she is meeting Friday with federal officials in Washington to discuss a grant that would allow the lab to reduce that backlog. Cunningham's blood sample was processed at the request of New York authorities who contacted the Vermont lab after learning state police suspected he was involved in the Dover thefts.

Cunningham awaits trial in New York for crimes more serious than the ones he is suspected for in Vermont. Nathaniel Seeley, a Windham County deputy state's attorney, said local police must do more investigation before his office considers bringing local charges against him. "It is largely unknown where this will lead to at this time," Seely said.

In Memory of JoAnna

"For God so loved the world that he gave his only Son,
so that everyone who believes in him might not perish
but might have eternal life."
John 3:16 (NABRE)

- The Boyle Road Band Program is proud to sponsor the JoAnna DeSilva Berggren Scholarship Fund. Thank you to all of the students and families who contributed.

- Thank you to the Boyle Road PTA for establishing the JoAnna DeSilva Berggren Scholarship Fund.

- Presented by Comsewogue Music Faculty — JoAnna DeSilva Berggren Memorial Scholarship Concert January 19, 2005.

- To the DeSilva Family, Hello. My name is Christine. I wanted to write to you to tell you how grateful I am that you have given me a scholarship in Mrs. DeSilva-Berggren's honor. She was an amazing person and really helped me achieve my full potential. I enjoyed very much working with her on the outstanding productions she had directed. I also wanted you to know that she has inspired me to be a music teacher. This money which I have been rewarded will not be put to waste. Once again, I would like to thank you for this great honor.

- A Bounce-A-Thon was held October 23, 2004, from 11:00 a.m. – 3:00 p.m. by the Parents for the Playground at

Boyle Road School. A special dedication ceremony took place in the field by the New Playground equipment – In Memory of JoAnna DeSilva Berggren.

- Let her memory and passion for the arts live on. St. Jude has set up a memorial scholarship in honor of JoAnna. Every year a graduating senior from William Floyd High School, pursuing a music degree, will receive a scholarship in JoAnna's name. Donations for the scholarship can be sent to JoAnna DeSilva Berggren, Memorial Scholarship, c/o St. Jude RC Church, 89 Overlook Drive, Mastic Beach, NY 11951.

- The International Star Registry renamed a star JoAnna Berggren – Star of Boyle Road.

- A parent planted a Cypress tree in honor and the memory of JoAnna Berggren. The tree was planted at a National Park in Israel. She wrote, "As I finished planting, my family and I recalled JoAnna and her wonderful voice. Her memory is now kept alive in a living memorial to her."

EVENING PRAYER
For
Our Beloved
JOANNA BERGGREN

Priest: God, come to my assistance.
All: Lord, make haste to help me.
Priest: Glory to the Father, and to the Son, and to the Holy
Spirit:
All: as it was in the beginning, is now, and will be forever.
Amen.

HYMN

O God our help in ages past
Our hope for years to come
Our shelter from the stormy blast
And our eternal home.

Beneath the shadow of your throne
Your saints have dwelt secure;
Sufficient is your arm alone
And our defense is sure.

Before the hills in order stood
Or earth received her frame,
From everlasting you are God,
To endless years the same.

A thousand ages in your sight
Are like an evening gone,
Short as the watch that ends the night
Before the rising sun.

149

A Heartfelt Thank You...

On Saturday the 31st of January 2004, our lives were tragically altered by the carelessness of a hit and run driver. As days passed, our family was comforted by hundreds of mourners as they solemnly stood by to say good-bye to our angel, JoAnna Berggren. Our grief was shared by JoAnna's friends, colleagues, students, and admirers. Although our hearts are filled with the pain of our loss, we take comfort in the overwhelming show of love and support we are still receiving.

It is obvious that our JoAnna was an extraordinary woman, who led a fulfilled life, and she will live on for years in the hearts of many – this is where we draw our daily strength.

We would like to offer a heartfelt thank-you to everyone, whether you brought food, sent flowers, gave us a card or note, shared a kind word, held our hand or hugged us – Thank you from the bottom of our hearts.

We would like to request these final favors in JoAnna's memory:

To JoAnna's students and choir: Remember her music!

To JoAnna's colleagues: Remember her passion!

To JoAnna's admirers: Remember her voice!

To JoAnna's friends: Remember her smile!

JoAnna filled a room with love and happiness; she lived each day to its fullest, always following her heart and faith. We ask that you no longer mourn JoAnna, but rejoice in her life – continue each day with her love in your heart.

Again, we thank you and may God bless you all….

JoAnna's husband: William Berggren
JoAnna's in-laws: The Berggren Family
JoAnna's parents: JoAnn and Bob DeSilva
JoAnna's siblings: Bobby & Rosalie, Angela & Bob,
Annmarie & Jimmy
JoAnna's nieces, nephews, aunts, uncles and cousins

We would like to extend a special note of thanks to:

Suffolk County Police Department
St. Jude Roman Catholic Church
Roma Funeral Home and the Kruk Family

Conclusion

"Let us not grow tired of doing good, for in due time we shall
reap our harvest, if we do not give up."
Galatians 6:9 (NABRE)

Sandi Huddleston-Edwards, Author

There are too few words to write that will be as beautiful as this
book of memories about a precious woman named JoAnna. After
all the interviews of shared smiles and tears, I feel as if I truly knew
JoAnna with her beautiful spirit and tireless energy. JoAnna was
a fearless and determined person more so than anyone I've ever
known or read about.

JoAnna found ways to remove any perceived obstacles and
remained persistent until her objectives were achieved. One of
her many lessons that touched my heart the most is to live each
day to the fullest. She knew that time is precious and fleeting; life
is short and sometimes ends too abruptly, without warnings or
chances to say goodbye.

Based on my own understanding, it seems that each day
JoAnna purposely sought out those who were sad or angry, hurt
or needy, disappointed or rejected to offer solace, help, hope, and
happiness. These are the people who hadn't already sought her
first. She didn't reach into her pocketbook and pull out money
that is easily spent and forgotten. She did it by reaching inside her
loving heart and pulling out beautiful sentiments of understanding
and acceptance.

She is said to have glowed. I don't doubt that. If you ever
see someone who is constantly smiling as JoAnna did and wonder
why, I think it's a sign that person's soul is overflowing with

passion and joyfulness, which can only come from knowing God. As a result, many lives are touched with harmony, peace, and the acknowledged mercy and grace, which comes from loving Jesus Christ. These people possess a life-long desire to live their lives as He did.

After reading the many cards, letters, and news articles, studying the children's drawings, admiring the handmade memory quilt, and hearing the heartfelt expressions of love , I truly believe angels walk among us. And if my belief is correct, then JoAnna was definitely an angel.

It is not difficult to fathom God sending special people to be guiding examples of goodness and mercy. It's easy to recognize those we deem as "good people," but is it easy to follow their leads? You can't read this book without discovering the many blessings people received because JoAnna lived. Her life had purpose. It's also interesting to notice the individualized messages each person received from her.

Over and over again, we're told about her beautiful smile that was given to everyone. She addressed people by name and cared enough to know people personally. She used her gifts of music, drama, and song to bring about peace and harmony around her and in the lives of others. Think about it. Because of JoAnna, a nephew and great-nephew want to take piano lessons. Former students and a nephew became teachers. Others became stage actors, singers, and musicians. Her brother-in-law wants to build theatrical sets and audition for roles. Church members, family, and friends share her inspirational life story with others so many may be brought to know God. A beloved brother has slowed his pace so he can appreciate his family and the world around him more. In summary, she influenced many lives who want to become more like her. I'm one of those people.

Because of writing this book with JoAnn and Bob, JoAnna has influenced my life, too. I'm honored and grateful God chose me as the author to write JoAnna's book.

Robert (Bob) Zippel
February 12, 1965 ~ April 19, 2020 (age 55)

It is with great sadness that Angela's husband, Bob, passed away on April 19, 2020, during the writing of this book. Angela and her children (Rob, Brian, and Samantha) and other family members have my sincerest condolences and prayers.

As you'll recall from reading this book, Bob was very close to his sister-in-law, JoAnna. He'd known her as a preteen who was a bridesmaid in his and Angela's wedding.

After the accident occurred, Bob accepted the extremely difficult task of identifying her body. Angela and Bob visited JoAnna's grave on special occasions and holidays. In addition, Bob visited her grave often. He seemed to find solace there and felt closer to JoAnna.

Bob had always hoped that when his time came, he could rest beside JoAnna. Upon asking the cemetery administrator if the grave site beside JoAnna was available for her husband, Angela was told it was, and not only that plot, but the four plots beside JoAnna. He was surprised that after sixteen years, no one had purchased either of those four gravesites.

So, Bob was interred where he'd wanted to rest -- beside his beloved sister-in-law at Mt. Pleasant Cemetery in Center Moriches, New York. The other three plots were purchased for Angela and her parents, JoAnn, and Bob.

Epilogue

"Blessed are they who mourn, for they will be comforted."
Matthew 5: 4 (NABRE)

This famous and comforting quote was written by Ralph Waldo Emerson.

"This is my wish for you:
comfort on difficult days,
smiles when sadness intrudes,
rainbows to follow the clouds,
laughter to kiss your lips,
sunsets to warm your heart,
hugs when spirits sag,
beauty for your eyes to see,
friendships to brighten your being,
faith so that you can believe,
confidence for when you doubt,
courage to know yourself,
patience to accept the truth,
love to complete your life."

This playground was created in memory of JoAnna and is located behind her music classroom.

This is a lovely picture of the DeSilva family at JoAnna's wedding.

Left to right, front row: Brother, Bobby DeSilva and JoAnna DeSilva Berggren. Left to right, back row: Sister, Angela DeSilva Zippel; Dad, Robert (Bob) DeSilva; Mom, JoAnn DeSilva; Sister, Annmarie DeSilva Marchisotto.

The children (students) of Boyle Road School made 169 quilt squares in memory of JoAnna.

The studenrs presented Bob and JoAnn with each quilt square in a large book on the day the playground was dedicated. This is a good picture of the book with the squares. The students made these squares in honor / memory of JoAnna.

Erica (left) and JoAnna (right). Erica was her best friend and in her wedding. This was taken in 2002.

Works Cited

Bittner, Fred. *Faith Gateway*. "Bible Verses About Happiness
  and Joy: Joy Comes When We have a Clear Direction fo
  Our Life." August 20, 2013. *https://faithgateway.com.*

The Compassionate Friends. "Time Has Proven that in Caring and
  Sharing Comes Healing." 2020.
  https://compassionatefriends.org.

Gein, Darlene. *Newsday*. "Long Island Celebrations." November 1,
  2003. *https://Newsday.com/long-island/celebrations.*

Guest, Edgar. *Family Friend Poems*. "Only a Dad." N.d.
  https://familyfriendpoems.com.

IrishTracy. *LI Weddings*. "They Found the Driver Who Killed JoAnna
  Berggren."March 15, 2004. *https://LIweddings.com.*

Joel, Billy. *Piano Man*. "Piano Man." November 2, 1973.

Kelleher, Jennifer Sinco. *LI Weddings*. "Mastic man accused in
  teacher's death." March 15, 2004.
  https://liweddings.com.

Kruk, Barbara Guarino. *Newsday*. "A Melody Too Sweet To Forget."
  February 11, 2004.

Longfellow, Henry Wadsworth. *Family Friend Poems*. "The
  Children's Hour." 1860. *https://familyfriendpoems.com.*

Naylor, George. *Family Friend Poems* "My Auntie." Oct. 2012.
    https://familyfriendpoems.com.

Scripture Catholic. "Sacrament of Confirmation." 2020.
    https://scripturecatholic.com.

Wagner College Department of Performing and Visual Arts.
    "JoAnna DeSilva Soprano, Junior Recital."
    May 2, 1995.

Wagner College Music Department. "JoAnna DeSilva Soprano
    in her Senior Recital." April 23, 1996.

Sandi Huddleston-Edwards
"For you, O Lord, are good and forgiving, abounding in steadfast
love to all who call upon you."
Psalm 86: 5 (ESV)

Sandi Huddleston-Edwards has passions for God, her family, and writing novels and memoirs. She holds a B.A. and M.A. in English and Rhetoric and Writing, respectively, from the University of North Carolina at Charlotte. She is a former adjunct professor of English and taught at Central Piedmont Community College, Montreat College, Johnson & Wales University, and the University of North Carolina at Charlotte.

As a freelance writer, Sandi wrote articles for *Lake Norman Publications, Tarheel Wheels,* and *Reader's Digest.* She is the author of two novels, an historical novel, four memoirs, a children's book, and two devotionals.

"I only write Christian genre. When I write, I write for God."

She and her husband, Barry, are the proud parents of three grown sons (Jeremy, Jeff, and Todd). They enjoy traveling and spending time with their two Yorkshire Terriers. They reside in Myrtle Beach, South Carolina.

Other Books by
Sandi Huddleston-Edwards

For more information or for orders, please go to
hearmyheart.net
or Amazon.com

Richard's Key
Roy's Sandman
A Stranger to Myself
The Clumsy Little Angel
Three Day Nights
Silent Victims
Hands Reaching, Hearts Touching
All for Him
You Can't Kill the Miracle
The Good Sheriff